The Permit That Never Expires

The Permit That Never Expires

Migrant Tales from the Ozark Hills and the Mexican Highlands

Philip Garrison

The University of Arizona Press
Tucson

The University of Arizona Press
© 2010 Philip Garrison
All rights reserved

www.uapress.arizona.edu

Library of Congress Cataloging-in-Publication Data

Garrison, Philip.
The permit that never expires : migrant tales from the Ozark hills and the
Mexican highlands / Philip Garrison.
    p.   cm.
Includes bibliographical references.
ISBN 978-0-8165-2831-8 (pbk. : alk. paper)
   1. Mexicans—Inland Empire (Pacific Northwest).   2. Immigrants—Inland
Empire (Pacific Northwest).   3. Inland Empire (Pacific Northwest)—Ethnic
relations.   4. Inland Empire (Pacific Northwest)—Emigration and immigration—
Social aspects.   5. Michoacán de Ocampo (Mexico)—Emigration and
immigration—Social aspects.   6. Garrison, Philip.   I. Title.
F855.2.M5G374 2010
305.8968'720795—dc22   2009034770

Publication of this book is made possible in part by
the proceeds of a permanent endowment created with
the assistance of a Challenge Grant from the National
Endowment for the Humanities, a federal agency.

15   14   13   12   11   10   6   5   4   3   2   1

Some of these pieces appeared as excerpts in a somewhat different
form in New Madrid: Journal of Contemporary Literature.

For Mrs.

Contents

The Permit That Never Expires

El Dolorgullo

Pera has what she calls la epilexia—and can't afford pills to control it—and last week she had three attacks. So early this morning, when she caught me standing in the Fred Meyer checkout line—me with three grocery carts of donated bakery goods—she got an idea. She wondered if I would write a note in English to her shift supervisor so she wouldn't have to work the grill. She'd mop floors, unload trucks, work anywhere that she wouldn't get burned if a seizure hit.

After I wrote the note, she tucked it in her billfold, tucked her billfold in her purse, and, while I gave her a ride to work, mimicked how the boss had steepled his fingers. Bring a note, of course. But no, I don't think you'd get burned on our grill. Probably slide right off, but sure, bring a note. Pera wasn't exaggerating, by the way. They talk like that here. El dolorgullo is what I call the resulting mix of pain and pride. Seeing humiliation endured in that intensely Mexican way, you feel pain tip over into pride, and it makes you remember your upbringing. Pera and I pulled out of the parking lot and merged into traffic. Another day of hard, oblique, Columbia Basin sunlight.

Pera studied the ventilator, then adjusted it. A mexicana immigrant— she gave a sigh—goes through changes understood by no one else but another immigrant mexicana. Learning to drive and cash paychecks, to register your kid in school. You read labels in English, you pay phone bills, and you navigate freeways. You work dishwashers and answering machines. And it makes you into a different person. Not entirely, of course, but somehow you don't fit where you used to when you visit where you grew up. The seizures were about the same, she responded when I asked. Siguen tumbándome y yo me sigo levantando del suelo. She got laid off at the potato shed. But Pera is equal parts fearless and heartfelt. Pera is about thirty, with a potbelly and a moon-shaped face.

And as to a work permit—bueno, she likes to say—el que nunca vence, the one that never expires.

Waiting in the Fred Meyer checkout line, with my donated bakery goods, I had been making small talk about the weather (hot) and the Mariners (a joke) with two young women named Jody and Sherry Sue. They wore Levi's and boots and had ponytails. They spoke with a twang that recalled their grandparents, Dust Bowlers and the like, from Missouri, Kansas, and South Dakota. Their grandparents formed a north-route counterpart to the Okies Steinbeck made famous and, like those Okies, found work in fields and packing sheds. Answering to German and Celtic surnames, driven by a suicidal pride, half-convinced that poverty was independence, their grandparents were people afraid of nothing but a vague shame they couldn't get rid of. Sherry Sue and Jody carried toddlers in their shopping carts, and cases of discount soda pop, and copies of *TV Guide*. Each was born thirty-some years ago in this valley, and except for quick vacations in Vegas or Yellowstone, neither ever left it. I know aunts and uncles of theirs. My kids went to schools that theirs will go to. The small talk bubbled.

At least until Pera eased into line. Buenos días, don, she purred. Pera, ¿qué ondas? Oiga, le iba pedir un favor, she grinned. She was worried about something. At the other end of the belt, Sherry Sue and Jody were scrutinizing their cash register receipts, looking at the floor, shooting their cuffs, and sniffing, certain that your author and Pera had begun talking about them. Without a syllable of goodbye, they marched to the parking lot, backs rigid, not even looking at each other, betrayed. That was when Pera wondered, would I write a letter in English to her boss?

Overall, the more it feels the effects of what I call im/migration, the more this town reminds me of where I grew up on the Mississippi River. No one ever forgot what the earth's primary feature thereabouts was. The gasping humidity, the limestone bluffs half a mile high, the dead-fish smell that hung over Front Street, especially the spring floods that got you out of school to lay sandbags—reminders came from all directions that life, your own everyday existence, was how it was because of that big green thing that ran under the bridge. Down at the other end of the river, there was exotic New Orleans, and French cooking, and jazz. But we lived on Mr. Twain's end of the river. We were plainspoken, reserved, and born to work.

Half a century later—the irony tickles me even now—I live beside another flow, one that connects the Columbia River Plateau to the Mexican Central Highlands. I'm talking, of course, about that current of words and feelings produced by the uninterrupted traffic in human beings that runs back and forth—but mainly forth—from Oaxaca to British Columbia. In other words, it runs from that steep platform at Monte Albán right up to the hayfield valley I sit in my backyard admiring. Spanish calls it el flujo migratorio. It is a current of immigrants and migrants, mainly mexicanos, that nourishes and sometimes threatens the place I live in now, gripping it in ways intriguingly like the hold the Mississippi had on hundreds of little towns along its banks.

Half an hour after leaving the supermarket, I am sitting in my backyard, on a cedar deck, and it is a godsend of a morning. A lawn full of dandelion puffs, and a breeze leaking through cottonwood boughs. The creek is so loud I heard it through closed windows! From a telephone pole, and the top of a cottonwood, and a barn roof, a few crows train what sounds like a running commentary on the scene. Their whoops and yips meet the background hum of a Weed Eater, a quail mating call.

But let me digress by admitting I don't do well with befores and afters, let alone plots and denouements, foreshadowing and irony. The truth is I live—like it or not—in a cobwebby present tense, having arrived at the age where time turns into texture, into something I move back and forth through. By which I mean that the merest whiff or glimpse is enough to transport a guy my age back over fifty years to a wink-and-nudge moment under blooming lilacs. That much is well documented.

People my age are as distractable as a house cat. Or we seem that way because, after a certain exposure to time, the mind treats before and after like any other border, as utterly conventional, an imaginary line between two languages that talk about pretty much the same place. My point is this. So what if I let events run together in the interest of texture? It catches the sneers and winces and whimpers that fly back and forth in these parts. It catches in particular the different borders imagined into place in local trailer courts. Benito Juárez and Marilyn Monroe. That kind of border.

Let me admit, as well, that both my family and my outlook come from Missouri, which is to say from border counties full of Bald Knobbers and bootleggers, the impromptu laboratory where bushwhacking was invented. Even though by now, in me, the violence dribbles off into footnotes and asides, I am very much the son of a land so divided that, during the Civil War, it had two state capitals and a star on both flags. I descend from impoverished ol' boys ready to die to (1) free slaves, or (2) defend the right of the wealthy to own them. All that freeing and defending mainly took the form of dry-gulching neighbors and cousins, plus any outsider foolhardy enough to show up, and finally each other, as their loyalties meandered with time, as happens in border country.

The birthplace of their attitude was itself a border, the one between Scotland and England, ultimate source of tent revivals and whiskey and the doctrine of the Inner Light. Hard work and the still, small voice and a hatred of authority. Earlier versions of me too ornery for even that wretched border got sent to Ulster—the border of a whole empire! It was at the Battle of the Boyne, in 1690, where stubborn, ragged, mainly rural volunteers in the service of William of Orange were first called hillbillies, a term the British troops of occupation were quick to apply to Scotch-Irish frontier families in Appalachia, some of whom wandered off and finally set up house—where else?—on a piece of that sullen border called Missouri.

I myself am about to retire from forty years in classrooms, from imparting a bit of backspin to the *Iliad* and Montaigne—most of my former students are by now middle-aged schoolteachers—and that is why I can sit here on a blue and windless day, a Wednesday morning in fact, with cottonwood leaves flashing, and my wife asleep in the back room. Why I can look around, lean back, and take in the entire morning. Sprinkler system to magpie to—ulp, the cell phone rings. Bueno? It's Pera, wondering could I give her grandmother a ride this afternoon while finishing my errands.

I make a note. I turn, well, to the very same air, a bit of white blown off the dandelions, but now I've lost where I was. But it was an eloquent interruption, no? It says worlds about the life I lead. Impromptu, ad-libbed, whatever you want to call it, my days in retirement swerve here and there with the luck, good or bad, of friends who live on the edge of what TV news calls the immigration problem, the couple of thousand mexicanos who make up a community in this valley, who nod to each other in parking lots, and who know the names of each other's kids.

I'm the age of their grandparents, you see, and they ask for advice when they get on each other's nerves. My friends are young, standoffish country folk, slow to trust, with long memories—but we go way back. I knew a lot of them when they were little kids. Years of distributing food—thirty-five tons a year to four hundred families—of interpreting, giving rides, lending a quick fifty. Vouching that fulano de tal is a guy responsible enough to be allowed to pay $800/mo for a leaky trailer—that kind of history is built up between us.

Look at the big picture. Mexico and the United States, fittingly enough, are separated by a river, one that wears a different name on each side—the Rio Grande, and el río Bravo. So it is no surprise to learn that what the U.S. government calls immigration is, for the government to the south, merely migration. So two rather different versions of the phenomenon exist, but no matter. Once you understand that immigration and migration, in most cases, are merely different phases in the same existence, you refer to the Mexican diaspora, and you prefer the term im/migrant. Overnight, in little towns around here, piso mojado signs appear on a supermarket floor, and tripe shows up in the meat case. And what about those who survive el flujo? Even those who settle down remain tied to it because of the jobs family members and neighbors have, not to mention an economy that thrives on throwaway labor.

We've all heard the guesswork. Maybe half a million people a year cross the U.S. southern border without documentation. One effect is that Hispanics—that highly contrived category the Census Bureau favors—are now the largest minority in the country. And other effects? Nobody knows. But a relocation of such proportions hasn't occurred in the United States since the early twentieth century, when the Great Migration North brought some four million southern rural black folks to northern cities, where they promptly became the dominant ethnic force in the century's culture. And it is not hard to see a transformation that deep at work all around us now.

El flujo migratorio—the immigration flow. Over the last century, it has been a regional and very nasty version of the Industrial Revolution, with peasants run off land they never owned and into mechanized labor elsewhere. By now, it breaks up families and destroys towns, but it also brings new towns—and, yes, new families—into being. It can be random, arbitrary, and wasteful, not to mention as cruel as any other force of nature. It kills people, it breaks hearts, and my young friends and I can't imagine the world without it. El flujo long ago became a fixture on our landscape. It is made of neither rock nor water nor wind but only of motion, of momentum. And yet, much more than any cordillera or watershed, it is the most compelling feature in the entire U.S. West and Mexican North. It imparts a peculiar spin of impermanence, nostalgia, ambition, and anonymity to life in the Mexican North and the U.S. West. It is our continent's internal Ellis Island, overlooked, unmentionable even.

Right from the start, el flujo admitted risk takers, favoring the patient and the ambitious, but it changed them forever. Mexican immigrants underwent something they never had imagined, a change so deep they noticed it only in details of voice, handshake, and timing. Collective wisdom soon decided they never went back to the ranchos they came from, and who knows? Maybe they didn't. But they certainly did talk. They told tales—always about el flujo, one way or another—clipped, flat, no-nonsense renditions of extremity. The people in the tales were hungry or plain itchy for excitement, or at least for another kind of boredom.

Understand one thing. My im/migrant friends are anything but helpless victims driven wherever demand takes them. To think so shows a serious lack of respect. Sometimes, in fact, they enjoy amazing successes. How often? I don't know. How come I don't know? Because, quite simply, there's nowhere to stand to see the whole thing at once. El flujo is a huge and shapeless and very sticky phenomenon that defies overall observation, much less prediction. It is human randomness in action. No wonder the scientific meaning of the word flujo is flux.

Motion free of direction, travel as a way of life—that is what el flujo imparts to the Mexican North and the U.S. West, what makes the landscape feel like nowhere else. A plain case of motion worship! Because most of it isn't fit to plant, the region draws nomads, draws hunter-gatherers and all their different descendants, including prophets and visionaries, glad-handers and rubberneckers, and runaways and honeymooning newlyweds, not to mention merchants, who in turn draw investors so mean they'd take a nail gun to a crucifixion.

An elderly fellow I know pulls in with a load of firewood I ordered. He pulls out the piece of plywood he uses as a tailgate. He digs a strapless Timex out of one pocket, glances at it, and proceeds to answer my question: Yeah, I wound up here. After I got to rodeoing as a kid. Got ribs kicked in by two different bulls, but I went all over. Rode in Madison Square Garden a couple times. He looks around, and his voice dangles over the edge of something. The truth is I went off rodeoing after I got back from Korea. Three years in Special Forces, and I couldn't slow down. When I couldn't quit dreaming about stuff we did in Korea was when I started riding bulls. Hell, I woke one morning, my whole bedframe was tore to pieces, but I didn't remember a thing. It was one night right here in town I quit rodeoing. The guy on the gate was drunk, and I was on a bull and damn near lost a leg, but the dreams quit right after that.

He pitches out the last scraps, throws the piece of plywood in back, climbs behind the wheel, and cranks the engine. When his window comes down, he wears a smile the Buddha himself would envy. You know, one bull, he had these great big horns, they stuck out front, but I rolled over real quick. Pausing for effect, he grinds a gear. So he drove 'em in right where I had been, and both horns caught in the ground, his own momentum broke his neck, and he fell over dead. The clutch shudders. The driveway is empty.

Everybody look out. I'm keeping a journal. I'm going to write down exactly what happens over the next few months. I'll be living at both ends of el flujo. The first four weeks I'll be in my own backyard, in the Inland Northwest, and then, for a three-week academic assignment, in an apartment in Morelia, Michoacán. In other words, the next year of my life will take place on opposite edges of that ten-million-person whirlpool that is el flujo. Get it? The daily lives of friends like Pera already wind through my own, though certainly not in any textbook multicultural pattern. When exposed to a lot of dailiness, after all, patterns evaporate.

The truth is, the lives of my im/migrant friends intersect my own at an angle visible only from both ends of el flujo.

From opposite ends of the twentieth century, from the lives of my im/migrant friends back to that of the homesteader who was my grandfather, there runs a subtle parallel, and it illustrates a brutal truth. When im/migrants say they enjoy a better life than what they had before they came, remember, it is the truth emerging, however obliquely. The suffering is both very real and a whole lot easier to describe than any sneaky, slow-growing sense of having bettered yourself. The whole thing is a real spirit-wringer. Talk about ambiguity! Notice that so much ambiguity calls for a kind of writing that tries to split the difference between the narrative and the thematic. In other words, these pages cut a diagonal path between (a) a chronological channel that runs deep, but narrows down to the individual(s) it follows, and (b) a certain thematic meandering to acknowledge the shameless variety of it all.

What qualifies me to write about el flujo, about those who ride it, and about those who fall off? Fifteen years ago, with a couple of friends, I began a food bank, a project that by now keeps me—twice a week, all year, face to face—distributing food to anyone who comes in the door, and 95 percent of them are mexicanos. Given a grant in 1999, the food bank conducted the local mexicano community's first, and only, survey, a document that has suggested a lot of my thinking about my friends, most of whom by now are veterans of el flujo. But there is another angle, of course. Think of molecules aligning. The truth is that my friends and I recognize each other from a long way off. How we do so is what this book is about. Think of it, for now, as a default setting we share, a kind of meta-attitude. Even diluted one part to a million, what we have in common comes across—a mix of élan, resignation, and something else, a sadness I don't have a word for, even though it clings like Cantinflas's pants to everything we do.

Maybe it's a nomad gene at work in my friends and me. After all, not counting a dash of immigration from Ireland and Chihuahua, my family history doglegs back to an eighteenth-century man baptized with what would become a regular family handle: Isaac. In 1776, at age forty-four, the ancestor in question plucked his North Carolina flintlock from the mantel and went off to shoot a few Englishmen. Probably the deceased turned out to be a bunch of sad, young, hungry grunts from Prussia, but North Carolina Ike himself lived to be a hundred. He died in 1832, on the green Kentucky farm that he had immigrated to only one year before. But the precedent was set. Most of us in the family are more subtly afflicted, I have to admit. Market surges and collapses—and wars both world and civil, not to mention revolutionary—are always available as pretexts. But after you see it enough in your own kin, you recognize that squirmy, un-killable impulse to hit the road.

Three Notes on Usage

To begin with, Mexicans have no ready-to-hand term for most of the thirty million souls who inhabit the country just north of them, calling them los gringos, or los güeros even. Certainly, the 10 to 15 percent of the United States that calls itself African American would reject those labels, but that community represents still another problem for Spanish speakers. Moreno is the term that refers to skin with a certain degree of melanin, but it's a relative term—one person being simply más moreno than another. Moreno lacks the knife-edge either/or distinction that English tries to make between black and white, a distinction that filled the history of the United States—the one that considers Washington, D.C., its capital, I mean—with tales of black folks passing for white. Meanwhile, in the United Mexican States, deciding whether someone is moreno or güero might resemble deciding whether a given day is hot or cold, cloudy or fair.

Second, the corresponding nomenclature in English is equally weak. English has no equivalent to mexicano—a term that in fact refers not to citizenship or place of birth, but rather to how the person in question thinks and eats and raises children, works and worships and blasphemes, treats authority figures and family members. A mexicano may be Chicano or Mexican or even—God help us—apparently hillbilly. After all, what is it I see when I look at myself? When I listen to my own speech, observe my own behavior, etc., I see a guy who passes through a mental turnstile several times a minute. But leave my self-observation apparatus running—for forty-eight hours, say, or seventy-two—and I observe a guy who seems to prefer the company of mexicanos/as, at least judging by how many hours a week he spends with them. It's nothing I observe firsthand. But when I look at myself as another person would, the preference is clear.

The reason isn't especially complicated, either. I simply find the company of mexicanos much less monochromatic, full of a wider variety of feelings, or at least of feelings more nuanced, of attitudes calibrated to finer degrees of tolerance. It probably has less to do with the message than with the medium, a broad and subtle difference between U.S. English and Mexican Spanish. Everything that, in the latter, sounds to the gringo ear so wholly redundant, so very baroque, so ingrown and finicky even—the endless shades that greeting and farewell take on; the con-permiso-and-buen-provecho element in everyday speech—all of it works like traffic signals between two people talking, indicating to each the type and degree of feeling in play. It isn't easy to learn, of course. The painstaking, fastidious nature of mexicano speech made Octavio Paz characterize the national way of life as a labyrinth of solitude.

The everyday talk of mexicanos features the tale, the old saying, the snappy comeback, and the ludicrous comparison. Precisely because it expresses so much of itself in tones that spin with counter-intent—audible only up close, in the original—mi raza remains what it is because of chats over back fences, or starched tablecloths, because of a heart-to-heart through a screen door, or a piece of mind delivered long distance. Listen for antique phrases, bits of speech that bear no information, only a vague goodwill to the hearer, a readiness to extend to him or her the rights and privileges of the civilized. Think of it as preening each other with words.

Which, by the way, brings up my third point of usage: how I myself grew up hearing the word hillbilly used. It was an acknowledgment Ozark people gave each other that, sure, most of the world thought we were hicks, and probably we were, but . . . Hunh? But! The oppositional conjunction: but! That was the flag we sailed under. We were chip-on-the-shoulder, long-term counter-punchers, specialists in the last word, the last laugh. Plus, we knew we were smarter than they thought we were. Finally, one generation—I think it was my mother's—took the word hillbilly and turned it inside out to where, depending on how they said it, you heard either embarrassment or pride, but most often a mix of the two. The history of the term hillbilly, in short, paralleled that of the term Chicano/a, which began before World War I as a sneer at ragged, illiterate country folk newly arrived from Mexico. Chicano, hillbilly—each is a term a later generation resurrected. Each can be brandished like a weapon, or like a flyswatter.

Doña Ermelinda Catches a Ride

The year she turned twelve, Ermelinda Jiménez de Suárez got her first job. It was mopping the tile floors in a huge house with china in a cabinet and a dinner table that seated twenty. Jilgueros hung in cages in every room. In the breeze that came through potted plants on the balcony, those birds let go a song that hurt your ears, it was so fierce. It rebounded off the damp tiles. It rolled back and forth, room to room, and it was beautiful—Michoacán was famous for its jilgueros!—but she left every afternoon with a headache.

So one afternoon seventy years later, Ermelinda recalls her very first job and looks out the windshield at where the Highline Canal snakes through sagebrush, half a mile off. A hawk glides. She is remembering. When she got here, the crowded, panicky discomfort she had felt on that first job vanished—overrun by weeks, and then years, of pruning and thinning and picking under Columbia Plateau skies. But the memory of her first job holds on like a cocklebur. Probably, by now, it represents her feelings about where she grew up, a childhood caught—and maybe no longer expressible—between those birds and that tile floor.

Ermelinda looks around. She's seen all this before. The sunlight slant, the stacks of empty pallets, the creaking of conveyor belts and Canada geese, everything says harvest time. Life in this town takes on a trance-like detachment. People enter that state of mind, built of repetition and sleeplessness, that preys on those who work twelve-hour shifts. They go home to a cabin or a trailer, door hanging crooked over cinder-block front step, mattress on the floor, phone numbers penciled on the wall. Random thoughts show up, dangling an attractive bit of wisdom just out of reach, and before long, supervisors tell each other the work crew is getting spacey.

In other words, this time of year will bend your mind like a stick in water. Even if you are, like Ermelinda, ten years retired from the freezer

plant, you get to thinking that somewhere else, out there in all that cobwebby time, the newlywed you is blinking and washing Sunday dinner
dishes. Blinking at a dish towel. Remember the freshly caught trout a
brother-in-law brought over for dinner? How was a person supposed
to know you had to cut the insides out? Then the landlord howling at
your screen door, all gray hair and neck veins, not to pour grease down
the sink, and the brother-in-law drunk sending a money order home pa'
mantener—he rolled his eyes—a la vieja y al sancho. The brother-in-law
with his hand on your leg under the table.

In other words, if you are Ermelinda, you sometimes get swarmed
over. You can get so delayed by the bits of resistance people call el
norte—or Out West, depending on what they leave behind—that suddenly it is years later. You're catching a ride out to your granddaughter's
house to babysit. When it all overtakes you, for a moment—the seventy
years, the birdcages, the tile floor—you flinch, look down a gravel road,
fold your hands in your lap, and clear your throat. Take the next left,
you say. The man behind the wheel smiles at you. Then we go straight—
you continue, deadpan—until a dog comes out. And he cracks up.

Now if you're the guy driving—and I'm the guy driving, who
else?—you turn left, pass between a tar-patch smell and a speed bump,
and you're there. Another parquiadero in another border town a thousand miles north of where the border was two generations ago. That is
how Pera's grandmother and I pull in with a week's worth of bakery
goods donated by Fred Meyer. And Carmen and Elida, Balbina and
Marbella—putting out tomato plants or walking the grandkids—walk
up and pluck bread from our car trunk. Plus a young gabo with shirt
off and a baby over one bony shoulder. A not-so-young gabo heaves out
of a lawn chair, takes a loaf, and says, much obliged. Doña Ermelinda
herself walks off with a smile and a sack of bran muffins.

Think of it. After a hundred years of researching hybrids and fertil-
izers, the country produces a scene halfway between the Second Coming
and a food fight. I admit I'm addicted to how it feels when nourishment
comes flying out of a car trunk in the form of bagels (raisin and plain),
French bread, muffins, Danish, donuts (glazed and chocolate), buns
(hamburger, hot dog, and kaiser). Loaves? Lord, yes. They boast ingredients of buttermilk or potato or granola, caraway seeds or dill, flour of
wheat or rye or bran, each loaf sliced, and in a plastic wrapper.

But get this. As if to remind me that what it contains isn't manna,
each wrapper closes at one end with one of those little plastic Kwik-locs

that made a millionaire of inventor Floyd Paxton, who lived in Selah, by the way, not fifty miles down the road. Ol' Floyd used to send an oil-voiced, revival-tent veteran, a Genuine Man of God, out to counter-leaflet United Farm Workers of America picket lines in '68, but I never met him. Floyd himself has surely departed the planet by now, but Lord, how rumors flew around among us sixties leftists. What was he funding? Everybody was sure he was behind that John Birch outfit. All our sixties backspin and bête noire–ing! It occurs to me, at this age, that Floyd probably thought of himself as God's repeat business. And viewed from here, that gawky fundamentalist faith he paid for probably was—as he thought—the finest thing he possessed. He died wondering how come nobody listened to a guy whose ideas worked at least as far as holding a bread wrapper shut.

So there. Under sunlit cottonwood leaves, while I shut my empty trunk, the world radiates these peeks and glimpses of another world. When I drain a coffee cup, clip a seatbelt, and turn right onto Canyon Road, every gully and gravel lane is twisted with other people's lives. To the south, the freeway runs through a potato field acquired by a county commissioner only days before the route was announced officially. This river bank is where a scared kid from Guanajuato put a couple of .357 rounds into an unarmed buddy. A puertorriqueña school-teacher drowned somewhere upriver while inner tubing. Picture, on yonder weedy island, a Sam Johnson scholar going down on a blonde accounting major. There even are local inner-tuber legends about floating this stretch the summer of '67 with the polished, touchy, evasive young Ted Bundy.

Eloquent Gesture

If you grew up in dry, rolling, huizache country—like my buddy Carlos—
tree planting in the Pacific Northwest took your breath away. Carlos had
never seen trees the size of what came out of the Cascade foothills on
logging trucks. He climbed and planted and climbed, and at every corner,
there was a backdrop to spin your head. The sierra went on and on. It
made you feel self-conscious and insignificant both, working with picture-
postcard vistas over your shoulder, peaks and glaciers and miles of what
mexicanos called, indiscriminately, los pinos.

Planting what were in fact eight hundred Douglas fir seedlings a
day, you entered a paycheck-to-paycheck existence. You fought loneliness with beer and CDs, hitchhiked fifty miles to weekend dances, paid
twenty dollars for a dozen Christmas tamales, fell in love with three or
four waitresses, and got a DUI—all in the course of adapting to life in
a land that inspired, flummoxed, and outraged a person. But the loneliness never let up. It went underground, then surfaced, depending on the
time of year, as well as on what kind of money you had in your jeans,
because relief cost money. Every time a nanosecond of loneliness leaped
out and broke your heart, you paid, if only via large bar bills and small
scrapes with the law.

At age twenty-eight, nearly six feet tall, Carlos Charles looked like a
guy used to waking in cheap motel rooms and walking through slash all
day. Was that his real last name? ¿Que qué? Nobody ever knew. Because
he had it all rehearsed. He was the son of a jipiteca runaway taken in by
a childless Kickapoo couple living under the Eagle Pass bridge, ¿y qué?
He had green eyes, brown hair, and eyebrows that bunched and twitched
every time he had a decision to make. Somebody said he did three years
in the penal because his mother turned him in as accomplice to the holdups that his kid brother was sentenced for. Amá had convinced herself
that her younger boy shouldn't do all that time alone.

The kind of guy Carlos was, he did his three without complaining, got out and headed north, and sent for his kid brother. It was a life that suited the younger brother very well. He was slender and good-looking and had a liquored-up genius for mimicking the accents of people, how they walked, held a coffee cup. But it was a talent that called for more restraint than he knew, el pobrecito, as one Saturday night—celebrating the end of a planting contract—it got him gut-shot.

Older brother Carlos, drunk, managed to load the kid in the bed of a pickup and took off barrel-ass for town, through seventy miles of high-desert Oregon, under a bunch of 3 a.m. stars. Until he ran out of gas, and the kid bled to death parked on a nondescript road shoulder under a big ponderosa by a creek. As light broke over a mountain pass, Carlos's eyebrows were bunching and twitching. He was sitting behind the wheel of a pickup beside his dead brother.

A local church agreed to ship the body home, so Carlos, the very next day, occupied the seat farthest back—curtain closed—on the first bus out of town. Couldn't bear to look at one more pinche beer-commercial vista full of trees. Heading east through sagebrush country, he thought about going home to Eagle Pass, but got off instead in a little college town and then—lightning rod for cheap irony that he was—caught on with a landscaping crew composed of out-of-work mexicanos. They gathered in the Home and Garden parking lot at dawn and went off in twos and threes with subcontractors or homeowners.

And the economy that had brought him here in the first place? It took the form of an olive green canvas bag with a shoulder strap. The bag held foot-long Douglas fir seedlings, five hundred of them, thick as a pencil, which got planted every six feet, or sometimes simply buried by crews behind schedule. They said that after swinging that hickory-handled hoe-dad for a month you could strike a kitchen match on your palm. The crummy, a rattly Dodge, carried eight guys, wearing T-shirt and flannel shirt, sweatshirt and jacket, three eggs and a pound of pancakes in the guts of each. Carlos remembered Bob, the Kentucky supervisor, corks and hard hat and shatter-proof bifocals, up and down slopes all day, whining, Let's take a little pride, or howling, Burn one. Bob was the first hillbilly Carlos ever saw up close.

Every morning they traipsed off, planting every eight feet, with Gary the blond-ponytail hippie in the lead, five years planting trees while he saved to study acupuncture. Gary lived in a tent, on peanut butter sandwiches, and split his attention between the *I Ching* and

Gurdjieff. Following Gary, an ever-changing cast of college boys and girls, out-of-work loggers, and young mexicanos still dazed from crossing the border. Finally came Walt, the skinny Tennessee foreman, dark haired, pale and toothless at thirty, who lived for planting trees and drinking wine. Walt it was who once described a cousin's vacation: she went to either Hawaii or Florida, the one you can drive to. Every morning in tin hat, suspenders, and ragged pant cuffs, over brush pile and stump, deer nimble, Walt paused at 10:30 for a small can of Polish sausages and a handful of snowmelt. It was dark when you left for work, Carlos recalled, and light when you went to bed, and weekends were for beer and anger.

One Saturday, his crew finished their biggest contract. They slept in a barrack, a tin-roof and concrete-floor dwelling, on cots lined up ten to a side, eighteen inches apart. After various cases of beer, by 3 a.m., the room smelled like dirty clothes, spilled beer, spoiled fruit, and farts. Through the screen-less windows, the creaking of frogs met the snores, gurgles, and whimpers that wound down through contraction and coiled into the secret-dreams division of each person. At floor level, a cot was creaking.

Carlos didn't need to open his eyes to know that his brother, in the very next bunk, was humping a certain chubby blonde who dropped by on payday. By the time he rolled over and looked, his brother was sidling up to the window at an angle and peeking out. With the calculating, impersonal gaze of a carpenter, the blonde turned to Carlos, ¿Quieres coger? Carlos flinched. He felt slapped. He felt invaded, then ashamed, then angry about the shame. Now an urgent note ripped through voices across the room, and now Carlos heard a noise like a book slapping shut and saw his brother drop. Carlos knew what had happened. But Carlos also was falling sideways, out to where a huge and not-quite-human something observed every molecule of him, every electrical impulse.

Who knows. Weeks. Months. Carlos shrugged, nodded, not even trying for words. After a blow to the spirit like that, well, Carlos went floating in and out. Everybody knew he lost his kid brother to a life of whores and drunks. Carlos squirmed a lot. Carlos was thinking ping-pong style, ad hoc, caught between himself and, who knows? somebody else.

His eyebrows went wild. He must've been on autopilot one evening, he said, walking back from some mini-mart, when he noticed a huge tent struck in a park, and a handful of men and women ambling toward it. He followed them inside, he said, and found the simple ingredients of belief: a generator purring, the smell of wet canvas, lightbulbs and moths overhead, heel prints in grassy mud, card-party folding chairs lined up. A hymnal on every other seat made it a place where the elderly whimpered into hankies about eternal things. Guaranteeing that life went on as usual, however, teenagers hung out in cars in the parking lot—with their lips locked on each other, and a fistful of underwear—dreaming of union-scale wages, snowmobiles, and Ski-Doos.

After a couple of hymns, the same guy with aviator glasses and tattooed forearms who greeted you at the door spent awhile beseeching and imploring, and then personal testimony took over. The tent was perfectly quiet. People leaned forward in those folding chairs, straining at every syllable. Here came a story made of fluorescent light and shifty memory, a daughter run over at age twelve by a Coca-Cola truck on her way home from school. Someone came back alive from Vietnam. Someone else went into remission. Somebody's grandmother got released from a painful body and gathered into glory. Another lady managed to shed fifteen pounds.

It made a lot of sense. Carlos was paying attention. After her own sinewy narrative nearly strangled a mother of four, and she collapsed, a large wave of impersonal blessedness hit that tent. Pity ran every which way, and people knew it was Jesus's forgiveness. It left a frizzy-haired woman gasping and grabbing herself. A fat kid quivered and closed his eyes, a drunk wept in the back row, the choir moaned an extra verse, and then people—blundering, anxious, hangdog people, and yes, including Carlos—stepped forward into a new way of life. God was watching. Carlos was sure. Since that night, he said, he felt relieved and free. But the way he said it made you think of a plastic wrapper blowing down a border-town street.

Dig up that spruce at the corner of 5th and Ruby—somebody told the landscaping crew Carlos was on, his first day here in town—then haul it off and plant it on the university campus right where they show you, okay? Bueno, okay, but that tree was fifteen foot tall easy. They dug all morning. Then loaded the tree, crossed a thoroughfare, went up a hill, and saw the building they were headed to. Then they got very quiet and stared through the windshield, blinking at the high-tension lines they'd forgotten about, lines they had to pass under. When they eased the flatbed up to the lines, the tree was at least three feet too tall.

Everybody collected around the flatbed, gaping at the power lines. Híííjole, somebody said when traffic began to stall behind them, and a couple of cowboys strolled up, and after them came a guy in a wheelchair, followed by two dogs. Dunno how to back that rig up, hunh? grinned Mr. Wheelchair. People always say that remark was what set Carlos off, although if you stop to think, his response would have been building for days. Who knows what crooked connection he made between his brother's death, amid miles of reforestation, and the single tree that had him, at the moment, stuck in traffic. For that matter, what would a fifteen-foot spruce mean to a guy from somewhere as desolate as what Carlos called, with a grim snicker, mi tierra. Anyhow, what he did was, he produced a fold-up handsaw, shinnied up that tree and—to long applause from the cars behind—topped it.

Talk about eloquent gestures! The deed caught the public eye for a moment. Four out-of-work backhoe operators down at the First and Last Chance Tavern drank to what they called a goddam Colorado Blue Shrub, and three "I told you so" letters to the editor came out, and all week those in line at the post office talked of nothing else. But the raw power of economics, of growers, motel owners, the local freezer plant—interests that needed a large labor force dependent on mainly seasonal work—that stuff formed the basis of what became, for Carlos, a pointed lesson in how the United States worked. Was Carlos paying attention?

The Expatriation of Esperanza López Andrade, aka Pera

At age four, she told people, she could read her older sister's first-grade books. And a year later—after a summer's exposure to tourist kids in the swimming pool at a Holiday Inn where her mother cleaned rooms— she decided she spoke English. And so one day, in English, with a Texas accent, she announced that she wanted to move to Fort Worth. The whole family laughed and cheered, then changed the subject. And yet it surprised no one when, on impulse, age seventeen, she took off with an older brother for el norte.

Once at the border, she wrinkled her nose at the thought of hiking even fifty yards through desert. Not her. She sent her brother off with a pollero and stepped into a restroom stall, where she put on the blue jeans and TCU sweatshirt she carried in a paper bag. Depositing her old clothing in a garbage can, she dabbed on a bit of makeup and disappeared into the crowd at the international bridge. By the time she got to the turnstile, and the INS agent behind it, a blonde couple from Dallas had put a name tag on her shirt and pinned her between them, they were so delighted at her interest in their congregation's missionary work. Years later, Pera's grandchildren would shake their heads. Granma Pera, all she had to do was look the agent in the eye and answer United States.

The near-ceremonial quality of Granma Pera's border-crossing story was pure invention. She had, in fact, entered el norte crouched behind the front seat of an old sedan. Why make a big thing of it? She rode up to the border making uneasy small talk with the driver, a glum kid from Sonora, a kid with bushy hair that reeked of marijuana smoke. When Pera rolled down a rear window, his response lagged, comically, maybe thirty seconds. Then he flipped a button, and the window rolled back up, and dark fields unfolded beyond the window. Pera tried to explain about the window. En mi tierra, she whispered, respira uno el aire puro.

Another thirty seconds went by before the kid growled, Y comen Uds. puro aire. The air where you come from is so pure you can eat it?

Pera was soon installed in the back room of her Aunt Pera's trailer in the Pacific Northwest, along with two cousins, ages fourteen and fifteen. Pera had always heard of housework as a way to make a living in el norte. So on her first day in the country, left alone for an hour, she promptly set out looking for housework. She walked four or five blocks to an apartment complex, noticed the new cars parked out front, and decided to try. She always had imagined tired, immaculate women thumbing books with titles like *How to Talk to Your Maid*, but wow, her very first day, a Friday, at the first door she knocked on, a woman in a pinstripe suit and lavender scarf squeezed Pera's forearm and pulled her inside. She plucked a tissue from a box on her desk, dabbed at one eye, and motioned Pera to an armchair. I don't suppose you speak much English? Pera smiled and shrugged. The woman stood and smiled and filled a kettle. You drink tea? Pera said, Of course.

The woman then made a lot of hard-to-follow remarks, alluding to a husband, a wedding, something about interest rates, and flying to New York, Houston, Miami. Pera stared at the rug so hard the nap blurred. When something about a biopsy and a dreadful diagnosis made Pera look up, the woman averted her face, picking at her words. Everybody thought his chemo was working, she said. Long pause. I left for Seattle, and they called right when I got there. Pera let the rug come back into focus.

The woman relaxed and smiled. She had been saying things she never meant to—at least that's what it sounded like. Another apologetic smile. I read somewhere that Mexican families, well, you know, wry smile. More tea? The woman sipped and cleared her throat. Her grandfather had made a fortune, she said, off coal mines and immigrant labor, and she wanted to get that out front, be perfectly honest about it, okay? But she herself, as a teenager, rode in a van to Tijuana to nail houses together and pray. And now she very much needed a friend. Really. Please.

It made no sense, Pera told herself. It also paid minimum wage. After all, Pera told herself, the woman might be observing some kinky form of Protestant penance. Algo es algo. The rest of the afternoon went by. That night, much encouraged, Pera retired to the back bedroom, only to find one teenage cousin in bed facing the wall with her heart broken, and the other suspended from school for writing her name on her boyfriend's face with a felt marker. Pera figured out from now on to skip breakfast and return after her aunt and cousins were asleep.

Pera went to clean that woman's apartment and knocked until her knuckles ached, and nothing happened, and next day the same. She put in a whole morning hanging out in the hallway. Finally, a guy in coveralls and a tool belt approached with an apologetic smile. She pointed to the woman's door and raised her eyebrows. The man rolled his eyes back in his head. In that draaawn-out voice universally known to make English understandable even to beasts of the field, he proceeded to tell her the lady was sorry, the lady had changed her mind. The lady wanted Pera to buy herself something nice with the twenty-dollar bill he extended while showing Pera the door.

Consider the year 1985. It was an unremarkable twelvemonth, full of what turned out to be a lot of disgrace and bad publicity. Ken Lay founded Enron that year, Mike Tyson debuted in Albany, and Mohammad Al-Fayed bought Harrah's. Pera knew nothing of all that, of course, but maybe—from a perspective far enough away to reveal which way the grain of history ran—maybe it was because she was born that year that Pera, at age twenty, found herself in a world that existed only when nobody was looking. You lay in a culvert covered with trash until dark, then went about your business. There were jobs all over.

There were distractions all over, too. At the supermarket, the newly arrived Pera really had to concentrate. Otherwise, her surroundings broke apart, fragmented into images of, for example, women's shoes, quick little life-forms: wedgies, flats, loafers and pumps, slip-ons, clogs and moccasins. The women above the shoes avoided each other's eyes, poking and sniffing and frowning, each acting as if there wasn't another human for miles around. Produce lay under mirrors, misted every few minutes, and people ignored each other.

Her first shopping trip, when Pera looked up and down the aisles for somebody, anybody short and brown, the aisles took off in all directions, shelves so high she couldn't see the top. Gadgets? Pera grew up fed from a kitchen equipped with comal and skillet, two pots, two knives, and a ladle. And here they had a special blade to peel potatoes. She walked around openmouthed at all that money in every direction. The money glittered and gurgled, honked and twanged and went thump. Overnight, everything got swept up or hosed down.

Her first week here, hired by a housecleaning crew, she grabbed a mop handle and let fly. She was sweating. Her arms and legs tingled with relief. On a TV set in the kitchen, Univisión, showing long lines and voter interviews, reminded her that today was election day on the other side. Words like comicios and mandatorio called up civics lessons in a cinder-block room in the rain. On the forty-eight-inch flat screen TV on a living room wall, to see a neighborhood that looked like her own, why, it felt like flying backwards. Her breath accelerated, her heart pounded, and she wanted to cry. Instead, she cleared her throat and attacked a coffee stain on the drainboard.

One evening, as she left work for home, it began to rain, and she ducked into the nearest store, its window taped over with butcher paper. The doorbell announced her. Fluorescent bulbs crackled. She looked up and down a long wall covered with racks of magazines and felt her face get hot. She tried to make her feet move the moment it took her to recognize, up and down the racks in front of her, one by one, full color, a tangle of arms and legs in gym-class postures.

The camera lens fell without mercy. It bared every inch of cellulite, every mole and ingrown hair, an inverted nipple here, a calloused heel there, a C-section scar. Above their fingernails and freckles, the models wore death-grin expressions. Pera flinched at the different colors of different body openings, shaved and goose-bumped and swollen, posed— all of it without one single feeling which she recognized, not one.

Even worse was the glance of the elderly man who turned from the magazine racks to her, ready to say something, and gave her a look that she figured belonged on the other end of a rubber glove: predatory, impersonal, peremptory. It made her ashamed of . . . she didn't know what. It made her feel like something limp and raw behind glass. After what seemed a very long time, the fluorescent bulb began hissing again, and her hand found the doorknob. It is fitting, here, to point out a certain feature of the situation that Pera misread entirely. She misread— however understandably—that look from W. W. (Suitcase) Rasmussen, who, at age eighty-something, merely glanced up from his study of a midget group-sex layout posed in French Provincial and saw this poor messican kid so embarrassed her eyes were brimming. He cleared his throat and started thinking about what to say in circumstances like these—he was a man of some upbringing, after all—but nothing came to him. And then she was gone.

The moment left a sour density in Pera. She was plain tired of men, tired of their wheedling and bullying and smug me-first reflexes, their lowered voices and flared nostrils, their shoelaces-tied-together loyalty to each other. Tired of husbands and fathers out of work and helpless, whining under pickup hoods with a six-pack. When she walked by, they would shoot her a look as good as said, May the Lord anoint your owies, m'ija. I bet I know what you really want.

Weekends, at las yardas, Pera was herself by now. Among rusty roller skates, a package of vacuum cleaner bags, a bottle of Roundup weed killer, a rayon shirt of the palm-tree-and-surf variety, she was herself. With the people she saw at these functions, she chatted like she needed to, even a word or two in English to elderly gringuitas who never missed a yard sale. Something about selling items in a driveway or yard, something about the arbitrary arrangement of objects with price tags, made life understandable.

On the Topic of Immigration

Tires crunch my driveway. Mole tunnels crosshatch the four truckloads of dirt we brought in to cover the glacier-ground rocks we built on. Five big sage plants are blooming yellow, and a morning glory vine slithers through dead ryegrass, and quail peck at roots. Walking up the driveway, waving, is a Peruvian exchange student, a journalist, María Angeles. Yesterday, she phoned wanting to interview me about the food bank two friends and I founded ten years ago. Ma. Angeles Gómez y Vasteguí, her card says. An unapologetically firm handshake.

Thank you for watching me, she begins—a little flustered?—I mean for seeing me. For talking to me. I know you are very busy. She's stocky, with a long jaw, and huge green eyes. Panty hose highlight the hair on her shins. Her clothing is tasteful and expensive. And from the look she trains on my ratty sandals and sweatshirt, ouch, maybe she expected a guy in a button-down oxford cloth shirt and polished penny loafers. She is, maybe, thirty.

I invite her to sit on the deck and drink a glass of ice tea. She produces a notebook and a mechanical pencil—maybe she's twenty-five—and clears her throat. Okay. How long have you been at the university?

Since 1967, I say, and wait for her eyes to glaze with the math of it, but she plunges on.

And how come you know Espanish?

I've been around it all my life.

Pardon?

Because of my grandmother.

Okay, she flips a page. And how long since you, I mean, she pauses, es de, esta obra de caridad. Maybe she's not too comfortable in English.

¿Hace cuánto que abrimos el banco de comida? I offer. She lifts a hand as if shooing a fly.

How long since you find it, found it?

Founded it, I want to say. But then I think, what the hell. About ten years. The eraser tip on her pencil quivers like a dog's nose.

And where they come from?

Our clients?

She nods.

From Michoacán, Jalisco, Guerrero.

Not Oaxaca?

Not many.

Are you sure?

I say nothing, and she crosses out the word Oaxaqueños. She gives me a calculating glance, and zas, I feel a Wal-Mart frame click into place around me.

And what do you call your own ethnicity? she asks. Chicano?

Nope.

Why not?

Because I wasn't raised as one. Because being Chicano/a leads to a very different kind of life from mine. Not better or worse, by the way, only different.

And what do you call the life you lead?

I'm a hillbilly.

A what?

It is simply another ethnic flavor, like Chicano/a, only different. Hillbillies come from border states and tend to be restless, hardheaded, anti-authoritarian, and loyal to their own.

Do they have an affinity for mexicanos, or is it vice versa?

It is both.

How come?

Well, because they're cousins. I mean their values are 90 percent the same. And when the two aren't fighting over scraps that fall off the table of the wealthy, they know it, and they act like it.

Hillbillies and mexicanos—I can't resist telling her—are going to be the prevailing mix hereabouts in the twenty-first century. Don't get me wrong. It won't be a seamless connection. We can count on scuffles and catcalls. But the values of Andrew Jackson and those of Benito Juárez are headed for a blend, not a collision, a mestizaje that'll knock your socks off. I pause for breath. Her pencil hasn't moved.

I know she's only trying to get an interview. But as usual, anything like prim disapproval, and my thinking balks and wanders. Suddenly,

I am ready to bet that María Angeles's literary future is already lined with triumphs and international praise. I mean, the fix is in. Without really wanting to, I imagine what will no doubt be her best-selling travel book, based on interviews like this one: the United States of cotton-woods and dandelions. Portrait of bilingual hillbilly on cedar deck. White-trash do-gooder. Am I pathetic or what?

She looks up and ¡ayyy buey! her eyebrows contract. And The Question follows. She would like to know, if it isn't too personal, how it was I got into handing out food? ¿Que qué? She closes her notebook. How come you do this? An artificial-sweetener tone. Ouch all over again. That is a very intrusive thing to ask. Why should I confide to her what feelings run between my friends and me?

So it is my turn for a calculating gaze. She squirms, but wants to draw me out. Maybe I would like to talk about world hunger? About how I see our food bank as part of a larger movement? Isn't it part of something larger? I flash what I hope is a killer smile. Think about it, m'ija. When I hand a bag of beans to my buddy Pera, what has that got to do with world hunger? It has to do, on the contrary, with matters a lot more local and momentary.

Ma. Angeles Gómez gives her head a perceptible shake, as if to clear it. But I press on. How come I hand Pera those beans? You want me to say she's got food-security issues? Remarks like the ones you want to hear misrepresent what is, in fact, a kind of intimate moment. Ma. Angeles's eyes widen, but I can't stop. And as to the issue of world hunger, I know perfectly well that what we do here is only a stopgap. You think when I take an aspirin that I'm pursuing immortality?

Ma. Angeles Gómez y Vasteguí, not surprisingly, asks another couple of questions, and makes tracks. And I feel silly. She wanted a feel-good interview with a noblesse oblige kind of guy, and I don't blame her. While we shake hands in the driveway, her jaw sets at a certain angle. Her new VW Bug roars once and pulls out smartly in the direction of town, leaving behind my lone notebook entry about her: that poor kid triggered a bit of antique Missouri nastiness in me. It makes sense, though. She was asking nosy questions—about feelings too complicated for easy description.

Me, I retreat to my deck. I sit down. I look both ways, as if at a rail-road crossing, and then extract a doobie from a shirt pocket, exhaling a moment later. Christ on a pogo stick! What endless patience is mine at the moment. And here, right on time, is my usual burnt-out love for the world, but more emphatic. Nail heads and blades of grass come into focus. Okay, let me admit that our local take on el flujo owes to our living at the start of the twenty-first century A.D. Because out here, where high-tension lines divert our power to L.A., and coyotes worry our garbage-can lids—hang on tight, María Angeles!—absolutely nothing travels faster than im/migration tales.

Let me try to describe what it is that María Angeles doesn't see, describe how a kind of belonging accumulates in someone like Pera. Start with what is the primal experience of el flujo: one afternoon, you find yourself transmitting silly signals with your hands. You're trying to figure out the word for parking place, or maybe the word for what happened between a dog and a flowerbed. Anyhow, your newly arrived next-door neighbor—license plates from Tennessee or Kentucky or something—shrugs and understands not a word of it, even though neither one of you can ignore certain likenesses. The same garbage bag full of Pampers; the same oil stain on the driveway. Maybe because each of you lives in a dwelling meant for wheels, for jackrabbit departures, you suddenly understand that the person you're signaling to feels no more at home in this country than you do, and never will. Congratulations. Your hillbilly neighbor and you just passed a kind of citizenship exam. Whether you call what you live in a trailer court or a parquiadero, you share a not-too-secret nationality, one that trumps any flag or currency or language.

☞   ☞   ☞   ☞   ☞

Here I am looking, next morning, at backyard impermanence, raw change in the form of bees and corn plants, the skunk under my deck, grosbeaks at the feeder. It isn't elegant or beautiful. It is awkward and embarrassing and urgent. But the older I get, the more I prefer the momentary. The vanishing act I share with a goldfinch outweighs every one of our differences. Maybe I better change my life.

Okay, cancel that call for a life coach. But at least I better apologize for how I treated María Angeles. It was a nasty lack of respect. Okay, how come I hand out food? Because, well, part of me believes that we share this world with certain ageless, immortal beings. They fasten on us, spirit attitudes, pungent longings which surface in us whenever, and however, they want. They change names and shapes at will. Nobody knows how many there are. But whoever walks down my driveway might be one of them. So, I try to live in a way that accommodates urges not my own, try to get nourished by chance encounters. And living that way, for me, involves the food bank María Angeles came to ask about. Una obra de piedad, it is. But Spanish gives the word piedad a resilient double sense.

It means pity, and at the same time, it means piety. Piety and pity? How could those two very different ideas share the same word? Well, maybe to suggest that they are a single attitude, or once were. Remember that Spanish, paralleling Italian, gives the name la piedad to certain depictions of La Virgen holding her son: a pose where empathy and worship are the same. In short, our reverence for the divine appears unrelated to our knack for feeling another person's misfortune. But is it? Maybe that reverence and that knack inhabit the same three syllables in Spanish because the language harbors the notion—and I think it does, ever so faintly—that to share someone else's discomfort is to acknowledge whatever created you both.

A quick trip to the dictionary, to the word worship: the root wor- is also the source of the term worth. Equally curious, though at a remove, is the suffix -wor, because it is the direction-indicating -ward of inward, forward, skyward. I think both entries make sense: to worship is to turn your attention worth-ward. I'm talking about the respectful recognition of, well, of what? Of what would otherwise go unnoticed. Because we lose track, this -wor, this little growl, lives way back in our throat. It refers to any object of our collective awe. Part of an extended family of words, worship is a cousin to weird and verse, to wreath and writhe and wrath. It is the inconspicuous neighbor of wrong, worry, wrangle, and wrinkle.

A breeze makes my nose itch. The tops of cottonwoods and willows squirm in the wind, and a sprinkler pipe tosses water on a pasture. Beyond are a twice-cut hayfield, four Guernsey cows, and a stack of straw bales, and beyond that a 1,500-foot basalt ridge with a canyon the river cut in it. The ridge itself—as most of them do in the western United States and northern Mexico—turns a kind of pink green at noon. As the day goes on, depending on whether I look through windowpane or window screen or plain air, it will go from rust red to juniper green. The sprinklers spurt. The cows gulp and chew.

The Life and Times of Ike Garrison

Because he was the kind of guy born to believe in larger purposes, Ike decided, in 1894, to put Republic, Missouri, behind him. He meant to seek his fortune out in Grover Cleveland's America—which wasn't at all a bad idea, apart from how it worked out. We have to consider the times. In the last ten years of the nineteenth century, it was new notions the country went wild over, not the fate of poor country boys. In 1894, the debuts of Cracker Jacks and Shredded Wheat drew more attention than the campaign of Jacob Coxey, who threatened to storm the nation's capital with one hundred thousand unemployed men, but showed up with only five hundred, and got arrested for walking on the grass.

The spring of 1894 hit with record-temperature lows and highs. By night, flowerbeds froze. By day, the parlor windows of the well-to-do flew open, emitting player-piano versions of two new hits, "I've Been Working on the Railroad" and "Sidewalks of New York." It all made a person aspire to own a parlor with a mail-order horsehair sofa, Persian rug, polished oak rocking chair, and sideboard. Anyhow, one day, Ike is boarding a train, checking his baggage claims, and guiding his new wife by the elbow to a seat. They stow a large picnic basket. They sit down. Maybe Ike is whistling one of the year's shorter-lived tunes—"And Her Golden Hair Was Hanging Down Her Back," or "O That Gorgonzola Cheese"—but certainly he has plans.

At that moment, Grover Cleveland was living proof of just how fast a man could improve his condition in this country. Three years after getting elected mayor of Buffalo, he found himself in the White House, where he promptly married a woman twenty-eight years his junior and begat Baby Ruth, of candy-bar fame. A lawyer with jowls and a walrus mustache, the president weighed 250 pounds, and snored, and suffered from gout. A century later, what we recall is Cleveland's indifference to popular discontent. He called up federal troops to suppress the Pullman strikers, after all, and left seven dead. But Cleveland was one tough bird, as well as a public servant devoted enough—when he noticed a rough place on the roof of his mouth, on the cigar-chewing side—to have half his jaw cut away in secret aboard the presidential yacht, so as not to panic the country during the economic jitters of 1893.

And now it was 1894. A thought balloon drawn above the nation this spring would include the recently closed World's Columbia Exposition in Chicago. People of Ike's generation saw it as a saucy response to the 1889 Paris Exposition, and especially to the Eiffel Tower. For a whole year, out on the shores of Lake Michigan, people studied that huge wheel designed by young Mr. Ferris, and frankly, something about it made you think. While it rotated thirty-six carloads of people—at fifty cents a head—264 feet in the air, offering a long look at Chicago, it also said something about getting to the top, and even more about staying there.

Anyhow, with his new bride at his side, and accompanied by his friend Bert and Bert's new wife, Ike left behind a Missouri town that now survives only in a handful of photos: clapboard, brick chimneys, front-porch railings. The train yanks and clanks, and then pulls out of the station. In a photo from three years after they leave, a young fellow about Ike's age balances—with mustache, knickers, and fierce concentration—on a bicycle that is teetering atop the rails in front of the train station. One sign says Republic, and another, 231 miles to St. Louis. Below the signs, hollow cheeked, in lace collar, muttonchop sleeves, and a felt hat with ribbons, clutching gloves in her left hand, the kid's mother fixes the camera with an iron gaze.

The train ride takes three days. The newlyweds cuddle and doze and, each time they change trains, check that their belongings get transferred. People talk in low voices about the Pullman Strike. Ike has a window seat, and what he sees makes him think of a stereopticon: steep, green, and shaggy, with creeks flashing around boulders, and towns you can't pronounce the names of. The newlyweds stretch and pace the aisle. They yawn a lot, and their clothing gets sticky. And the Wild West? A train station of striped awnings, with Indian blankets for sale, pottery, painted bows and arrows, shelves of books, magazines, produce, and candy. When they finally arrive, and stand on the board sidewalks of Sandpoint, Idaho, it takes an hour for the train sway to leave their legs.

With the Great Northern Railroad completed only two years before, it is likely that Ike and Burt worked at the Hummingbird Mill—though not a single document exists to prove they did—which was running two shifts, with more than two hundred men, producing cedar electric and telegraph poles. Steady income would have reassured the two young couples, although as to civil society in Sandpoint, we have the word of its mayor: it was the toughest place in the United States. Photos from 1894 do indeed feature the new Sandpoint schoolhouse, complete with a bell tower—please ignore the raw stumps out front—but, my God, who would want to teach local youth? Not after the winter when local youth decided to create a pond for a skating party, and stuffed and flooded the town culvert, and then ripped up the board sidewalk for bonfires. And the adults were worse! Sandpoint had six whiskey dens and was famous for what the locals called lynching bees.

About the time Ike and Bert arrived, workers digging a water main unearthed four corpses, including that of a red-haired woman. After much investigation, an elderly local recalled what had happened. One body was that of a fellow who entered a saloon and, bigod, fell over dead, which event the redhead grieved till it triggered a quarrel with her lover, whom she promptly shot, before slugging down an overdose of morphine and whiskey. And the fourth corpse? Some guy shot through the heart during an unrelated gambling disagreement. These were the years when a traveler described Sandpoint itself as four dozen rude shacks and a dozen tents, surrounded by homesteads and railroad land purchased for $2.60 an acre.

Everyone knew about the loneliness of homesteading. Surely that was what prompted Ike and Burt to build their houses side by side. They dug a well, hung a bucket on it, and set out rearing their families on fresh venison and a vegetable garden. Idaho, for Ike, was a slow-motion paradise, the hunting and fishing so good he would recall it with tears—a world war and a half century later—dying on a sofa in a daughter's living room a mere twenty miles away from Republic, where he started.

Ike's story was a classic. He hit the road in hopes of a life more like the one he wanted, a practice equally common among the rational and the squirrelly. No matter what the body's circumstances, that still, small voice in a person frequently opts for elbow room. Call it being contrarian—on my part—but let me emphasize how that still, small voice in people like Ike is famous for being very hard on those around them. And by that I mean that you better remember that any im/migrant story bears a turning point, a fulcrum, the moment after which nothing is ever the same. Frequently unnoticed by onlookers, it marks a change you yourself may recognize only when onlookers point and giggle. Or maybe they grimace, when that fulcrum slips like a noose. From way off here, in the twenty-first century, we recall what Mark Twain, another Missouri boy, wrote about the piece of American history he and Ike shared: it was the Gilded Age.

Watch out, by the way, for the word American, that dactylic hangnail on the language. It ought to refer to a person from any one of the three Americas, North and South and Central, right? We definitely need a word like that. But listen to how Mexican immigrants—even their native-born children!—go around calling the hillbilly neighbors Americans. They believe that they themselves are, and always will be, mexicanos, ¿y que más da? Their unshakeable faith awes me. It recalls a Dust Bowl cousin of Ike's, a farmer foreclosed on in the '30s. He looked around after the sheriff auctioned off all that he owned and said, Lord, it would of took a miracle.

A hangdog neighbor said, Well, maybe the Lord let you down.

Fiddlesticks! Wouldn't be a miracle if it happened every time.

Course not.

The cousin's remark expressed the kind of resignation that brought Ike back from Idaho after only eight years homesteading. What happened made a story as brutal as it was brief. One day, one of the children vanished, a little girl, and the frantic parents were sure she'd fallen down the well the two families shared. They lowered a ladder and groped for the body and found nothing. When the kid finally came toddling around a corner of the house, the two families exhaled with relief, but only twenty-four hours later, Ike's wife contracted pneumonia and died within a couple of hours. And only hours after that, Bert's wife succumbed to what her death certificate called sympathetic pneumonia.

Even from a century away, the tale wears a splinter of coincidence: the child is feared to have drowned, and the next day the mother dies with her lungs full. But is it only coincidence? Here's another version of the tale. The widow of Ike's younger boy recalls that, years ago, the family decided the two wives had probably died of something contracted from their drinking water. The two friends had dug their well, the story goes, without allowing for Idaho's more porous soil. Probably their own outhouse killed those poor women. Nothing will do but our two country boys pack up all four of their children, speechless, and hop a train back to Republic. Years later, somebody would recall the two fathers and their kids trooping back to the baggage car, each time they changed trains, to make sure their belongings got transferred.

Like so many who mourned the passing of homestead life, Ike was born too late for the classic West. Consider the buffalo herds. The year of Ike's birth, 1873, saw a million and a half buffalo killed—according to ex-buffalo runner Frank Meyer—but the very next year, only 150,000 were killed, and production plummeted even lower in the years that followed. Ike probably felt cheated—who can blame him?—felt that a cruel coincidence had robbed him of both the woman he loved and a taste of history. Not to mention the guilt for the death of his wife. Ike probably spent his last forty years knowing that outhouse, or his location of it, killed his wife. In time, he would've felt his private grief for a dead wife blend with the whole country's nostalgia for something it could barely remember, until they were nearly the same.

More than a century after Ike's death, it falls to me to collect these scraps of family history, a grandson living in times so like the Gilded Age I can't resist the gravitational tug of all that falsehood and jingoism. And that's not all. By the kind of homely irony common to these tales, I live not far from Sandpoint, Idaho. In a slightly different version of the tale that overtook Ike, I moved to a town founded by turn-of-the-century settlers who gave local roads their surnames—Pfennig, Rasmussen, Tjossem, the last sometimes pronounced "t-jawsome." The whole generation of them answered to nicknames like Horsepower and Middlepig. They settled in places they named Badger Pocket and Hungry Junction.

At 7:30 a.m. at the Kittitas Mini-Mart, locals hunker down in baseball caps, swilling coffee and bitching about the snow pack. Word is, the Bull brothers got six million for a couple hundred acres. The speaker pauses with creamer midair to emphasize what needs no emphasis at all, not to guys tired of calf pullers and hay hooks and bank loans, and tired most of all of pretending they aren't. Nobody says a word. Behind them, however, two mexicano grade-schoolers lined up at the video games rack are speculating.

Oye, wonders one, what you think would happen in a fight between Superman and Mighty Mouse?

Estúpido, the other sneers. It could never happen, que Mighty es de cartoons, but El Súper, well, es un vato, he's a guy!

The grandparents of those two kids were probably part of a migrant stream that ebbed and flowed with the agricultural seasons, thousands of people moving through a yearly routine. Many began with winter vegetables in Arizona, and then went on to calculated combinations of asparagus and cherries, pears and apples and peaches, all of it proceeding, more or less, by agricultural seasons. My friends who live in el flujo today, however, are caught in something a lot more flux than flow. Their lives vibrate with a kind of molecular movement.

Agriculture employs many fewer people now. Instead, in today's counterpart to the crop-following life, my friends nip back and forth across the region, and sometimes the whole country, from one poorly paid job to another. The relative simplicity of following crops has given way to a complicated networking, one that may propel a person from swabbing Las Vegas motel toilets to nailing shingles in Phoenix, from washing cars in Seattle to bussing dishes in Atlanta. A single migra raid or factory shutdown throws ripples in all directions. The difference between migrant and immigrant—between native- and foreign-born, documented and undocumented—is very real. It is a great advantage to be legally employable. But the monotony of the work overwhelms a lot of those differences.

The monotony, and the impermanence. The turnover in el flujo is breathtaking. A researcher in 1967 marveled at the number of sudden departures, as well as at the motives that occasioned them, from a weekend binge to a dustup with the boss, from a husband's roving eye to insinuations about a daughter's conduct. But you can imagine. While a family of five pulls out at 3 a.m. owing a month's rent, the fruit tramps who sleep under a bridge blame unemployment on the college boys and the spics.

Maybe the economic desperation that drove the labor camps of forty years ago does, nowadays, sling a worker from one end of this republic to another, but there's still never enough money, and most of the people you get to know still vanish without a trace. El flujo is by now a vast and bristling network of opportunity and/or exploitation, depending on where you look. It is intercontinental in ways nobody ever imagined. And the main constant over the last forty years? El flujo still resembles a traffic jam, where a whole lot of what is hillbilly intersects with even more of what is mexicano.

⁊   ⁊   ⁊   ⁊   ⁊

Impermanence, nostalgia, ambition, and anonymity—those are the primary colors of el flujo, but they nearly always pinwheel into something quirky, and maybe even kind of holy, you never know. My favorite flujo tale is that of Willie Keil, who rode the Oregon Trail from Missouri—where else?—out to the Pacific Coast in 1855, despite the fact that he was dead. Willie had succumbed to malaria while his family was packing, but Willie's father, the Reverend Keil, founder of the Bethelite sect, meant to keep his word to his son. So he had Willie's lead-lined coffin filled with hundred-proof Golden Rule whiskey, then nailed it, caulked it, and took off right on time. Outside Fort Laramie, when a handful of Indians approached, demanding to see what he had, the reverend let them peek inside, and they fled. Six months after the family left, arriving right on time, the reverend planted his boy in what is now Menlo, Washington.

The Keils were smart to flee Missouri when they did, by the way. Ten years later it was hell. After Appomattox, it attracted dozens of young men armed and ready to get famous. In the main square in Springfield, ten years after Willie died, the young James Butler Hickok dispatched a certain Davis K. Tutt with one shot at seventy-five yards. It was a heartfelt response to the insolence the latter had shown by wearing Hickok's gold watch—in public, no less!—after winning the thing the night before in a card game. Once returned to the proper vest pocket, that watch would tick off eleven more years, plus eleven days and a few hours, before Hickok sat down at a poker table in Deadwood. They dealt him that hand of aces and eights, and he slumped into history, having in the meantime been both interviewed by Henry Morton Stanley and, briefly, on the New York stage with Bill Cody.

⁊   ⁊   ⁊   ⁊   ⁊

The original Homestead Act took effect January 1, 1863—the very same day, fittingly enough, as the Emancipation Proclamation. A century and a half later, though, we tend to value each document more for its good intentions than for its concrete effects. Lincoln's proclamation freed no slaves, after all, not in the literal sense. No, it took two more years of slaughter, and ten more of bitter reconstruction, to ensure the blessings of liberty, etc. And as for the Homestead Act, well, over the course of its 124-year history, more than 2,000,000 individuals did file claims, but fewer than half of them—only 783,000—ever obtained deeds. Homesteading survived a lot more vividly as a topic of conversation than it did as a way of life.

But wait. Let me own up to my sources. It was his older son, Joe, at age 84, in 1989, who wound up dictating much of Ike's history. From the porch of a big house overlooking a lake in Kansas, with his younger boy installed in a big house beside him, and the older boy a minister in St. Louis, Joe began pouring his life into a tape recorder. The leather-bound typescript of his remarks, privately printed, would bear the title, in simple gold lettering, *JOE*. He could just see it. Born in 1905, he weighed thirteen pounds and looked like an egg, so they gave him the middle name of Oval. Just imagine. On a screened porch, retired from a successful accounting firm, mournful, gregarious, close mouthed, Joseph Oval Garrison recalled the grotesque poverty that had stalked his father—beginning with a scene one night on the Fourth of July. Ike is with his brothers. They're digging a hole in the yard of their rented farmhouse. They've brought a mule, a wagon, and kerosene lanterns. The air is thick and wet. Because it is July 4, from half a mile off, beyond a bonfire glow, you can hear a lot of speeches about freedom. Ike and his brothers keep on digging.

Notice that the place is rented. Ike would rent nearly all his life— the Brittain Place, the Sukow Place—but Joe writes like he's never heard the word sharecropper. Once, in the Cherokee Strip, Ike had the bad luck to lose three hundred hogs to cholera, then a tornado blew the porch off the house. One spring, Joe writes, Dad was too sick to plant, and neighbors showed up with twenty-five teams of horses. While they plowed his whole 160 acres, then harrowed and seeded it, he watched from the porch. The wheat looked good when it ripened. So one Sunday, Dad headed for the barn, ready to harvest, but Mrs. Eaton, the owner, told him no working on the Sabbath. So Dad sat back down on the porch. That afternoon he watched hail wipe out the whole crop.

Joe emphasizes his family's isolation from the world. For example, the only remark of Ike's concerning politics to survive was the regret he expressed on the day his first daughter got married. When the preacher arrived ninety minutes late for what was supposed to be an 11 a.m. wedding, Ike wished aloud that his daughter could have been married under a Republican president, but now it was past noon, and Woodrow Wilson held office. Six years later, no one even knew what to say when a stranger rode up with a hundred head of cattle. The guy kept fretting that he wouldn't sell them the next day in Republic. The armistice had just been signed, he said.

Religion only intensified the isolation. Even though the family claimed to be of Huguenot stock, by 1894 it had long ties to the Campbellite sect, a belief that demanded an itchy, personal relationship with God. Ike descended from people who knelt and prayed when they felt the urge. People of iron faith, of no patience at all with imposed dogma, they were followers of Alexander Campbell, a nineteenth-century pacifist. But after three generations of theological hairsplitting—between the Disciples of Christ and the Christian Church and the like—the faithful were downright fractious. Poor people demanded passion from their faith after all. Later generations might wince, and moderate what they could, but faith was changeable and explosive. Whatever its local affiliation, the underlying faith that Joe was born into thrived among border dwellers. A faith calibrated to leaving behind, to living on the edge, it appealed to the poor and the pushy. Long before it crossed the Atlantic, it was the scrappy faith of tent revival, shouting, and tearful repentance.

Joe recalls attending a Lambert, Oklahoma, church until a fistfight broke out between two choir members. At the time, a lot of school buildings were sitting vacant in wheat fields, he writes, after the district consolidated. So Dad and Uncle Bill and a group of people got twelve of them free, just for tearing them down and leveling off the land, and started a new church.

Joe was the first person baptized. When I came up out of the water, he writes, my sister Leora wrapped me in a big blanket and drove me in an open buggy north into a cold wind three miles home. Anyhow, I asked her, a couple years ago, Leora, I said, how come you didn't let me dry off? She said she didn't know. But yes, she said, it happened exactly like that. Joe concludes with the news that, years later, he detoured through Lambert to show his wife the church where he got baptized, but she got the last laugh. Now it was only a wheat field.

The isolation took a heavy toll. Joe recalls moving around a lot.

I don't remember how old I was when we sold everything we had and loaded our belongings on the baggage cars of a train to Howell County, Missouri, as Dad was going to farm the Mark Brittain Place outside Republic. When we got there, we found the house full of oats. So we sacked them, took them to town, and sold them, and had a three-room house, with a big fireplace in the living room. The owner, an elderly gentleman, used to bring out a stool and watch us milk or weed his garden. Every week, right in front of us, he plucked the *Katzenjammer Kids* out of his Sunday paper, and tore the comic to strips in front of us. In those days, Dad made extra money by breaking broncos: when hitched to the walking plow, between two Percheron bays, its halter tied to each, the bronc lit out and pulled the plow by itself until it was ready to ride.

Finally, all their wandering seemed to end. Ike and his family bought their own place. When I was thirteen, writes Joe, Dad took our money out of a box under the loose board in front of the fireplace and made a down payment on eighty acres, a mile and a half north, with a year-round spring in the middle of it. From our house on out twenty miles south, it was nothing but woods. Here and there a clearing held a rotted log cabin, little spots of blue grass around it with flowers in them. Or we'd be plowing corn, and a shower would come up, and we'd go squirrel hunting. We used to coat our hands with honey, and let bees crawl on them, and follow them to their hive. I ran sixty rabbit gums every morning before school. The entire world was our toilet, and we didn't send Christmas cards.

Then Mother got sick and we sold the place, Joe writes. She wouldn't live long, the doctor said, so we headed back to Republic. I sat at one end of her Red Cross cot in the baggage car, and Dad sat at the other with a monkey wrench at his feet. A fellow with a gun strapped on came through the baggage car and said we couldn't stay there. Dad reached down. No, he said, we're staying.

That was an example of the self-control that Ike had learned that Fourth of July night, when the neighbors were off hearing speeches. He learned it while sweating, whispering, passing a kerosene lantern, backing a borrowed wagon up to a hole in the ground. He had to learn it. Six months before, during a smallpox scare, Ike and a brother had broken out all over. They spent several weeks quarantined in a niche in the smokehouse. The first of many cruel coincidences in Ike's life brought him out of the smokehouse on the very day that his father died of a heart attack. Public officials, fearing contagion, wouldn't let the body of Ike's father cross the county line to be buried next to his wife back in Republic.

Apparently, Ike was ready to go to war. His brothers relieved him of his shotgun, pleading with him, instead, to help bury the old man a foot deep in the front yard. And so tonight, six months later, they were proceeding to re-bury the body right next to their mother's grave, hauling off excess dirt in the wagon, covering their work with bluegrass sod. Five years went by, and they even put up a tombstone. By then nobody cared. Joe displays a masterful touch, by the way, in noting how the brothers, even while elaborately honoring their father's body, didn't cause themselves any more digging than was necessary.

Joe's ironic detachment probably owes to his being the child of Ike's very unhappy second marriage. Immediately on his return to Republic— only nine years after he left on the great adventure of his life—he married Amanda, a spinster, six feet tall, who quickly fell victim to her predecessor's good looks. Poor Mandy. By now, only aging grandchildren recall her, a bony, fretful, timid, domineering creature. It is her old age they remember, naturally, years after the family assigned her the role of sour, self-hating, second-choice wife. And by then Mandy gave a great performance. Mandy was well attended to in her old age. Her primary caregiver was a stepdaughter, the one who never married after a fiancé died eating her fried chicken. Next door to her widowed daughter, Mandy lived with her drapes closed, and neighbor kids avoided her driveway. Mandy spoke in a whine, dressed in nightgowns and bathrobes, and could see in the dark. One day when the daughter wasn't quick enough with a pan of warm water, Mandy crossed the yard and appeared in her living room doorway, tottering, almost bald, to announce that never mind she had took a cold-water enema.

And yet, surely even Amanda, when she married, must have hoped for a happier ending, for a marriage other people would envy. When Ike proposed, in 1903, Amanda was a thirty-year-old spinster with glasses and a big nose. Maybe it seemed a dream come true, to marry a nice fellow with two little daughters, but maybe not. Her wedding photo reveals a tall woman slumped as if to fit herself into the picture frame. She appears to be sneezing. Over the next seven years, Mandy bore Ike a boy and a girl and then, at age forty-one, after bearing another boy, she started having dizzy spells. One time her eyes rolled back, and she grabbed the clothesline, and laundry blew all over. Other times she burned dinner, or put in too much salt, and the two older girls practically raised that baby boy.

Over the years, the consensus arose. Mandy was nursing a venomous envy of Ike's dead wife, but who knows? Certainly Mandy reared her two stepdaughters with such indifference that when one of them, dying at ninety-two, left a twenty-page note in her will—in blue ballpoint ink, printed, all capital letters—to say her stepmother was a bitch, nobody disagreed. After all, people remembered, no sooner had Ike bought that little farm than Mandy announced she was dying. She came home from the doctor's with a terminal diagnosis: her insides, he had told her, were all stuck together, and she hadn't long to live. So she insisted that they move back to Republic, where her family was. Then she went to bed and lived another forty years. In a photo of her visiting Ike's grave, she stands with feet planted wide apart, shoulders slumped. A stepdaughter's handwriting on the back notes that Mama said to tell people she had to stand this way to keep from falling over, ha ha.

It was 1941 when, on a daughter's living room couch, heartbeat weak and irregular, Ike died with a smile halfway between satisfied and resigned. The family gathered around him had gone to the restroom, for a moment, or was answering the phone, when the younger boy—people called him Little Ike—came bounding up the front stairs and caught that smile and felt his own life swerve so hard that—forty-eight years later, on his own deathbed—he'd whisper to a doctor that he really wasn't afraid of dying.

Joe, the narrator, simply cannot resist a flashy digression. But who am I to talk? And yet, you know why I keep winding Ike's story through an account of Mexican migrants from the Central Highlands? Because, in the long run, they share a remarkable talent. They know how to avoid time, or how to ignore it, I should say. Like the fellow in Walden who let eons go by while he was carving a walking stick, Ike and my friends—most of them, I mean—know how to disappear into the present, without fuss, into a work that would drop them to their knees with tedium if they let it. But they don't. And that is where what is hillbilly intersects with what is mexicano. What family members admired about Ike is his taciturn resilience, a virtue that mexicanos acknowledge as el aguante, forbearance.

People like my mexicano friends and Ike inhabit another dimension. Their lives demand to be judged by a parallel procedure, one based not on triumph or defeat, but rather on endurance, on outlasting. From Aristotle's remarks about the hero—plus a couple of thousand years of similar thinking—Western Europe and its heirs contracted an emotional disease, a self-destructive preference, one that takes conflict more to heart than it does cooperation. It celebrates triumph—or defeat, even—but never plain perseverance.

Let folk-hero movies illustrate the difference. Whichever Hollywood incarnation of him you examine, Billy the Kid goes down to a showy defeat. The episodes click into place and produce the only outcome we will accept. Garrett pulls the trigger, and the Kid is no more. Nothing could be clearer, or more final. Now contrast the Kid with another folk hero, a fellow vaguely parallel, but wholly mexicano. Gregorio Cortez merely survives. But he does so in a way that emphasizes his perseverance, his willpower. He has a ferocious equilibrium. He outlasts five hundred Texas Rangers and endures a stretch in prison, emerging pardoned, unbroken in spirit, only to resume a quiet life with his wife and kids.

Ike Garrison was that kind of guy. He had a spirit balanced enough to keep on getting up in the morning. He wasn't notable, distinguished, unforgettable. He was ordinary in all but his talent for endurance and modesty. Packing up and moving back to Republic, for a second time, now to prune other people's apple trees for the rest of his days, he held onto a view which admires not triumph, but rather, well, whatever keeps us coming back for more bad luck or betrayal. Think of admiring a character with a genius for bare survival the way the Aristotelians admire a hero's struggle. Now and then we all admit a distaste for the heroic, whatever form it takes, with Homer and Shakespeare featuring loud, rich people whose fortunes soar and collapse in rather predictable patterns. We can learn to appreciate that stuff. But daily life trumps anything heroic. It has a tighter grip.

Adventures in the Old Country

My last academic term before retiring, I get room and board and a regular U.S. salary to live in Morelia, Michoacán—half a day's ride from where I used to live in the Mexican highlands—while teaching a single course to eight students: readings and field trips. Like the Migration Studies Program it is part of, the course aims to familiarize monolingual-English youngsters with el flujo migratorio, a lifestyle they come across mainly in the form of gardeners and housekeepers and parking lot attendants.

Quantitative studies of immigration are everywhere, of course. Anyone with Internet access accumulates in a couple of hours more hard data about it than is gathered by all but a very few of those who dwell in it most of their lives. In other words, as far as el flujo goes, facts are cheap. It is the feelings connecting those facts that are hard to come by. The readings and field trips acknowledge that students can't, or don't, imagine life in el flujo, the pure randomness of it, the conflicting claims it makes on a person. The field trips and readings detail the feelings released when immigrant Mexicans negotiate the largely hillbilly U.S. West.

As in past terms, the program will put me up in a house under a big green hill bearing a water tower and a brushy ravine. Fifteen two-story houses of pastel stucco line each side of the street, each with a newish van or economy car parked in the yard, black water tank on the roof, tejas on the front-roof slope. Stucco colors run from burnt orange to sky blue to lemon yellow, and concrete power-line posts march off in each direction. Where the private street meets the city avenue, the drawn chains and a small guard house announce that this is a gated community. Out back, above a dusty vacant lot, the slope shoots straight up. Eucalyptus tips, marbled clouds.

Years ago, I tried to ride local combis—public transportation mini-vans—but I stepped on people, and lunged, and felt like a fool. After that, on every trip, I meet two or three taxi drivers a day. Typically, a cabbie will say he pays 200 pesos/day for the cab, plus another 100 in gas, so he's gotta make 500/day to feed his family. Imagine that he wears a three-day-old beard, is missing an eyetooth, and puts in sixteen-hour shifts. He may point out big, shaggy brown hills already subdivided to house the thousands of people from Mexico City who show up to sell contraband clothing or to open a taco cart or, yes, to drive a cab. The taxistas reinforce my prevailing opinion about people from the Central Highlands: they are like no one else on the planet. A tribe given to winks and overtones and sly asides, they know they constitute a drama both hilarious and wretched. And they can sense which one—of all the foreigners passing through—is ready to appreciate the show.

I feel at home in Morelia because El Salto, Jalisco—half a day's bus ride away—happens to be where my feelings for Mexico touch down, a landmark I visit after long stretches in the United States. Every one of my immigrant friends has a place that works the same way, his or her own fixed point, one that maybe even no longer exists, though it remains a default setting, and keeps the distance elastic, even if some of my friends go back only in their heads. Probably, any stable point in your feelings would have that effect. In my life, that point is El Salto. The name means waterfall.

Curiously, every time I visit Mexico—after a grace period lasting from twenty-four hours to six weeks—I begin to remember why it was I left the country the last time. Qualities like unpunctuality and corruption come to mind, even as I acknowledge that my critique owes to expectations acquired in el norte. Before long, every time, I start to feel a simmering impatience with Mexico. And what is worse, it always feels familiar.

Last time, the day I got to Morelia, I visited a downtown department store hunting for socks. There was no one on the entire floor but three young women salesclerks. Chatting languidly in a corner, they barely acknowledged my entrance. I waited and wandered a few minutes. Not a one of them looked up. In fact, they treated me the way salesclerks used to treat what we nowadays call people of color in the finer Kansas City department stores of my youth. But hold on. These kids weren't bigots. No, they were valemadristas, youngsters screwing around at tedious jobs with no future. They spent what they earned on what they wore. Each was no doubt the proprietress of a hair-raising fantasy life. Gossip was their main release. Why should they notice some elderly güero who was apparently lost? But sooner or later, all my empathy wears off, as if a warranty has expired. Suddenly I couldn't care less what I sound like to these girls! ¡Que muy poca seriedad! ¡Bien incumplidas Uds.! And just as suddenly, out on the sidewalk, I notice headlines full of the same character flaws the world always has attributed to Mexicans. That is when I figure I must be ready to go back north and start missing this country again.

This term, after two planes, a van, and ten hours sleeping without a twitch, I wake to the Venetian—please!—blinds, and then prowl. I walk two blocks for beer and ceviche at Sanborn's, then back to bed with the copy of *Songlines* left on the credenza in this house, the very one that I shared with the wife I'm already missing. After only thirty-eight hours. Where's that Chatwin-style notebook I bought to scribble in? Restlessness is fundamental to human well-being, says C., and who am I to doubt, tucked in three thousand miles from the beloved. Okay, I got it. At rest or at risk, our innards take over, and we head off and hunker down. Enough said. How about those four plump women travelers at the Houston airport back from a cruise, comparing cabins, cuisine, skylines, and vowing to each other their whole existence had changed? On TV, a taxista says that night before last he was assaulted and lost his watch and five hundred pesos. Hear the hopeless anger in him? La colera que quiebra al hombre en niños. That city map is thumbtacked on the wall exactly where I left it four years ago. There are a framed Diego Rivera reproduction, a shelf of other people's paperbacks, and icy tile floors. Out the window, the power-line posts are waiting, the private street, the guard house and chains. Maybe I'll wind up, later, missing life in a gated community.

Our first field trip is to Plaza Valladolid, to catch an appearance by Subcomandante Marcos. These are the closing months of the hottest presidential election in history. Aside from his role as spokesperson for the Zapatista movement in Chiapas, Marcos is actively waging what

he calls La Otra Campaña, an eloquent rejection of the three exist-
ing political parties. A year ago, in a famous communiqué, he wrote
that all three were a sham. One, the PAN (Partido Acción Nacional;
National Action Party), he dismissed as the party of nostalgia—nostalgia for Opus Dei and the Cristero Revolt, for the society page and
bourgeois etiquette, for Maximilian and Carlota and Elton John, for
what he calls that Sunday aspirin dispensed from a pederast's pulpit.
For afternoons of bridge and canasta, for the Knights of Columbus and
burned ballots. The PAN's slogan might as well be: Mexico is history
tucked away in a convent.

The second party, the PRI (Partido Revolucionario Institucional;
Institutional Revolutionary Party), which ruled the country from 1930
to 2000, represents grand-scale fraud and theft, students and teachers,
the murder of workers and campesinos, neoliberal economic policies,
the repression of labor unions, and history as propaganda. The PRI's
slogan ought to be: Mexico is a whore ruled by the hardest dick. The
PRD (Partido de la Revolución Democrática; Party of the Democratic
Revolution), the third party, is a family business disguised as a political
party. It represents turning over the Zócalo to showbiz spectaculars,
importing a zero-tolerance doctrine to punish young gays and lesbians,
expressing indifference to resistance and liberation movements in other
countries, and working with the PAN in some states, and in others with
the PRI. Its slogan ought to be: Mexico is nothing more than a budget
in dispute.

So here we are at Plaza Valladolid. The students disappear into
a sparse crowd. Fountain drops splash my notebook page, etc., etc.
El grupo Nomás Esclavos is blaring. Two guys are selling balloons,
Michoacanos, short, wide of body and nose. A teenager with hennaed
hair and a limp goes by. In moustache and big straw hat, a campesino—
sombrerudo, bigotudo—carries a hammer-and-sickle banner for Poder
Popular. Sweat drips on my page. Marcos waits in fatigues and his
famous ski mask, hands clasped behind his back, emitting smoke puffs
from that famous pipe. Dignitaries introduce a Purépecha group, a student group. Marcos waits in the hot sun, impassive. At 1:15, plaza one-
third full at best, a speaker rails, a woman reads a prepared text. Es el
mismo sistema, says a campesino from Santa Clara. Two pigeons circle
the plaza, bank, and perch across the street on a roof, over a balcony,
where a girl leans on an iron railing, a newspaper folded over her head
against the sunlight.

Marcos speaks, in a clear and mellow voice, three minutes max, noting that differences exist among those of La Otra Campaña, pero nos hemos unido, etc. Left-hand salute, clenched left fist, camouflage cap, black mask, and black Levi's tucked into boots, he puts his hands in his pockets. His sentences get longer, denouncing the three main parties' presidential candidates as the Three Little Pigs. No estamos pidiendo una limosna, nosotros, nosotras, hay otro Michoacán, uno de muchos colores, gracias compañeros, compañeras. By 1:45, it's all over. The crowd strolls off to military march music. That guy oughta lose the mask, a cabdriver remarks, pues it could be anybody up there. Well, yeah.

ʓ ʓ ʓ ʓ ʓ

Two weeks into the term, things go wrong with the class. The day after we saw Marcos, the students ambled in the door in twos and threes—fifteen, no eighteen minutes after we were scheduled to begin—so I posed a question. Think about Marcos, I said. Not long ago he was the world's most famous Mexican. You saw him wait patiently for an hour while a handful of nonentities finished addressing a skimpy crowd. How come he did that? The students shrug.

We don't see what you're getting at, one says.

I'm getting at the fact that he could have waited out of sight in the shade. I'm getting at what people in this country call el respeto. By standing there, Marcos conveys a simple respect for the existence of others, an acknowledgment that their time is worth something. Consider it a meta-attitude. You have to exhibit respect before Latinos will hear anything you say. This country runs on el respeto, and/or the lack of it, so learn to be on time. A hand goes up impatiently.

Yes?

Isn't four books an awful lot to read for a class like this?

In the discussion that follows, one student cites the long lines in clinics and banks and the like as proof that Mexicans really don't mind waiting. Another changes the subject.

Isn't it true that Mexico exhibits less cultural diversity than the United States? Up there we recognize dozens of different ethnicities, right? While Mexico is nothing but Spaniards and Indians.

I wonder, for an instant, how would Socrates handle that remark? The discussion swerves to include beaches and discos and happy hours. And I'm shocked at my own reaction.

It was thirty-three years ago that I first taught U.S. college students in Mexico. Nixon was still in office, and Mexico was rich with petrodollars. Currency devaluation, political scandal, unemployment, and cost of living hikes—the list of misfortunes that followed is well known, and since then, one academic term after another, I've guided field trips and graded exams and tried to make sense of the near-collapse of a great country. Student interest has varied over the years, depending, more than anything else, on the powers of empathy any group of individuals arrives with. Ten weeks in Mexico changes forever the lives of some students, while others never should have crossed the border.

In this group, alas, I meet an arrogance I've never felt before. Most of them have had some contact with mexicanos employed in the service sector, with waiters and housecleaning personnel and the like, or have managed to volunteer a few hours at day-care centers and food banks. It was a contact that, however flimsy, has combined with intermediate-level Spanish proficiency to convince them of their own expertise. They develop an unflappable, callow aplomb. The interviews in one of the textbooks, they sniff, don't sound like real Mexicans talking.

On me, their arrogance has a kind of a zero-gravity effect. The greater my astonishment at their pretensions, the more an equal but opposite astonishment makes me doubt my own thinking. Maybe my view of immigration simply isn't understandable. Maybe I'm out of touch with the world they live in. Could it really be that eight different people are turning, on the country and its immigrants, the unadorned disinterest that I hear week after week? I need another approach. I invite guest lecturers. I show interviews videotaped with immigrant shopkeepers. Then I invite the students, two by two, to lunch. Nothing changes.

ℨ   ℨ   ℨ   ℨ   ℨ

In a house that shelters one U.S. academic after another, year after year, I brew ice tea, and sit in front of a floor fan, and turn sixty-four. A blue Post-it note attached to the top of the living room wall says techo, roof. Llave says a yellow Post-it over a water faucet. The one stuck to a lampshade says lámpara. News flash? I'm an antique schoolteacher is all. As specialized as that Argentine fighting dog they finally bred so mean the males and females fought each other instead of mating, and the damn thing went extinct. I am not exactly otherwise employable, owing to a widely noted testiness of manner. How long have I been at it? Somewhere

I have stashed a bundle of freshman themes written exactly two days before Jack Kennedy got shot. That dog, by the way, was el perro de pelea Cordovés, of which not even a single photo survives.

I treat myself to a birthday stroll in the park. A young zoo lion sleeps surrounded by six lionesses, on his back with eyes closed, mouth open, about a yard of pink tongue dangling out. He's vain, lazy, bored, condescending—all the traits a young guy is said to need to get along behind bars. A tiger paces, a jaguar curls and growls, but Leon's attitude is built for doin' time. Even when occasional amorous advances on his part end with his getting his ears boxed, he shrugs and goes back to sleep, no doubt to dream of better things, a larger cage, more females.

The Gigante supermarket across the street shut down a week ago, leaving a Sanborn's and a megaplex movie house at opposite ends of walkways lined with tributes to a recently-risen-but-once-again-plunged economy, shops selling haircuts, electric appliances, shoes, dolls, makeup, plane tickets, hand-care products, soccer uniforms, first communion dresses, candles, beads, foot-care products, ice cream, perfumes, costume jewelry, skin-care products, girdles, camping equipment, swimsuits, cell phones, knickknacks, musical instruments, espresso, hamburgers, candy, video games, all of it hinting—like the life-size cardboard movie stars propped and hung and taped in place—a life more satisfying than any imagined by these head-swivelling teenagers. Watching three kids in uniform unload plastic bags from an armored car, I see them shoulder three or four bags each and lurch toward a bank in the shopping center. Each wears a revolver, a crew cut, and a wary look. Bullets sparkle around the waists of two, and the third wears a belt of shotgun shells. A small door slides open behind the passenger seat, revealing more plastic sacks. Can't tell if they know the shopping center is dying all around them.

≥   ≥   ≥   ≥   ≥

The last field trip is to El Calabozo, pop. 1,100, a rancho so isolated it has no telephone service. Eighty percent of the males aged eighteen to fifty work in el norte, returning for only a couple of weeks at year's end. That is no doubt why doña Tomasa introduces herself and begs me please, please, to use that Google satellite–view thing to check whether her husband—he vanished across the border three years ago—has started another family. Doña Arnolda says that bureaucrats of the fifth level demand attendance at weekly meetings unannounced beforehand. Accumulate three absences, and they cut off your kid's scholarship. Both Sras. agree that people from the side of the river that is green with trees and milpas don't want children from the other side—all dirt, nopal, maguey—attending the public school.

And me with my own attendance problem. Out of eight students enrolled in the class, only three have bothered to come. I'm pretty sure most of them still couldn't say why Marcos waited through all those dreary speeches. Failing this completely at work I've been doing for forty years is surprising. Instead of embarrassment or regret, what I feel is relief. I feel like a guy retired from asking people to imagine feelings that they've never had. Whew. Ya estufo. No more explaining oblique attitudes about eroded hills and rust red cow paths. About pothole highways that swing by towns with unpronounceable names. About a certain tree in the Arizona desert where polleros hang the underwear of their rape victims.

A True Account

It was from El Salto, Jalisco, that I set out, half a lifetime ago, on a wild goose chase so intricate I haven't got to the end of it yet. And I don't expect to. For reasons soon to be apparent, I never told anyone about it—about that weekend, I mean, not that I really felt the urge to. My wife, for example, who knows me down to the molecular level, has no idea what went on out there. My reticence about it owes to the primary understanding among the three of us who went off together. We were never, ever to discuss what happened, except with each other. But I haven't seen those other two guys in more than twenty-five years. Maybe what happened that weekend explains how come, even three thousand miles north, I gravitate toward people from the Central Highlands.

Let me begin with a little history. That weekend was part of a highly involuted moment in Mexico's history. It was an era of kidnapping and peso collapse and bullet-riddled sedans, yes, with the Guerrero highlands full of armed men and women, either freedom fighters or bank robbers, depending on whom you asked. It felt like the eyes of the world were on Mexico, and a few people even worried the government might tip over. But me, what did I do? I went on a pilgrimage. From my compadre's house in El Salto, I set out on the kind of ritual journey you take to give thanks or to ask a favor.

What gets to me, especially now, is how neatly the idea of pilgrimage contrasts with that of el flujo. A pilgrimage is symbolic right from the start, while im/migration may become so, but only in retrospect. Im/migration tends to erase the past, while you undertake a pilgrimage in part because so many before you have done it. Each phase of a pilgrimage contributes to the end point, while im/migration recognizes no end point at all. On and on. My own little pilgrimage revealed a lot of personal loose ends, of course. It isn't a flattering angle on your author.

I flinch at my own knee-jerk reactions, my perma-antagonism toward power. I try, by now, to think of that weekend as a needs assessment.

Anyhow, my one and only pilgrimage began at a Guadalajara cultural institute, where I taught students—or tried to—how to write about themselves, about each other, and about Mexico. The staff was from all over. Working there was a guy they called Julio el Huicholito, who taught yarn painting: plywood coated with beeswax, with swirls of colored yarn pressed into it, forming figures. Julio explained that the figures represented plants, animals, weather—whatever conditions prevailed the last time the yarn painter traveled to San Luis Potosí. By which he meant the end point of a famous pilgrimage Huichol people make.

Beeswax and yarn, in the hands of the adept, produced an image that pinned you down, stopped you in your tracks, told you something about how brief life was—but only an adept had hands like that. Without a pilgrimage behind them, the figures were only so much yarn and wax. Anthropologists came from all over to film the embroidered shirts and pants and feathered hats of a pilgrimage they were sure remained unchanged from pre-Hispanic times. Julio shook his head at how he was taking money from college kids who had never set foot in San Luis Potosí.

Anyhow, one night, Julio showed up at my place, hat in hand. He looked like he was waiting for an answer. Talk about surprised! How did he know where to find me? He shook his head, then shook hands impatiently. No thanks, he didn't want to step inside. He merely dropped by on his way to the bus depot, he announced, bearing an invitation to a pilgrimage he was making. How about it? Was he serious? I was packed in five minutes, leaving a note that said, well, that the huicholitos came and went when they thought best. One bus ride led to another, and another. Then we caught a train that ran once a day from a town named Charcas (Puddles) to a village named La Maroma (Somersault). There, we three pilgrims got off and started walking, Julio and me, plus the twenty-year-old nephew he brought along.

Get one thing straight about Julio. There wasn't an ounce of Noble Savage in him. He watched TV and spoke fluent, if accented, Spanish. He sent his kids to public schools, and even had them baptized. No chance you were ever going to confuse him with Carlos Castaneda's Don Juan. On the contrary, Julio was a guy in his thirties, with a wife forever unhappy, and in a line of work apparently as ephemeral as that of essay writing. Everybody said he knew his stuff, that Julio could talk all night about ancient lore, that he answered questions about his faith with aplomb. With me, however, he talked about the price of yarn and how to cure colic. Somebody else might've heard his remarks as parables, but after twenty-four hours on that bus seat, well, to stretch out in front of a campfire was to forget.

Julio and his nephew sat cross-legged on the ground, with me self-conscious and sprawled on a blanket. Bien zancudo Ud., the nephew grinned, how long my legs were, as Julio took out a half-size violin, worn and stained, and tucked it under his chin. What followed sounded like bagpipe notes. It certainly wasn't soothing, but I caught myself nodding, then leaned back, looked up, and felt all that night sky. I fed the fire scraps of huizache, an empty cigarette pack, a sardine-can label.

Oye, Julio finally said, ¿si quieres esta sabiduría? He was talking to me. His question snapped in the air. What he wanted to know was, did I really want to see the world though eyes like his, to make a habit of it, to become a regular pilgrim? Hmmm. It was an honor indeed, but one which would involve, year after year, buying bus tickets and food for maybe as many as ten people. But hold on. Julio and his family lived in a single-room, dirt-floor, cinder-block, twelve-by-twelve cabin. They shared a toilet and faucet with fourteen other cabins. Why shouldn't a well-to-do friend offer to buy food and tickets? Okay, but for how long was Julio going to expect this? Seriously, how long? But sure, it was tempting.

Julio's calm won me over. The weekend before, he had taken a group to watch his cousin debut as a professional wrestler. We sat in a tin-roof shed, on bleachers, among a few dozen huicholitos, all come to town for the weekend, and wrestling fans every one. Most wore the traditional bleached-cotton blouse and pantaloons—loose, embroidered with geometric designs—and some wore hawk feathers and ribbons. Arriving an hour early, passing a plastic jug of mezcal, they nearly fell out of the bleachers with glee when the dressing room door crashed open and Julio's cousin—also in blouse and pantaloons—sprinted out and vaulted into the ring, 110 pounds of backflips and flying kicks and face paint and war whoops.

Given the notion—common among anthropologists—that Huichol people avoid conflict, I noted how Julio sat through the whole thing with a pleasant watchfulness. Finally, nothing would do but to ask him. Did the huicholitos believe that his cousin's rage was the real thing?

Oh, sure, he said. On impulse, a follow-up question—did he believe it too?—followed by the elevator lurch of having asked a stupid question. He had given me the very same look of amusement he was aiming across tonight's campfire at me.

So, what did I want to do? Of course I wanted this kind of life. I felt myself shrug. Why else would I be out here in the middle of the desert at night? The nephew laughed, but Julio just nodded and went on chanting, scraping notes from that battered violin. It got cold that night. While Julio sat there in shirtsleeves, the nephew and I wrapped ourselves up in blankets and shivered. By daylight, after leaving gifts— mirror, chocolate, ceremonial arrow—Julio set out hunting peyote.

The trick is to pay attention, he whispered. Ignore your hunger and thirst and tiredness. You stay awake long enough, every huizache plant and shadow says something different.

As for me, I figured I better act like I did this every day. I gritted my teeth to keep my mind blank. I felt silly. And then I hit a transparent door. I felt newborn; I felt peeled. Spider, breeze, coyote, cloud, whatever crossed my path inflected my sense of direction, and zas, peyote cactus looked exactly like its pictures, a little gray-green asterisk in the dirt, and no big deal. When I sawed off that squishy root—used the key to the very office an institution of higher learning provided me—the first taste was mushrooms. Then it foamed like hydrogen peroxide. Twenty steps later, every discomfort vanished. My feet and my backpack got very light. And yet, I felt that doorway before I saw the plant, not after. I wanted to remember that.

Alas, nothing more happened. Walking back to the railroad tracks, to await the train, I let myself admit that I had expected more. How about a squared-away finale, at least, a vivid end to things? Here I was headed back to pure anticlimax. Was this another bit of deadpan Huichol humor? Right then I learned you should never believe anything you hear about visions. I felt like a guy in a shaggy dog tale. My vision, well, it was of the tunnel kind. Three guys were walking through the desert with lighter steps, spitting now and then, each with a birthday-party smile on his face.

So far, the weekend illustrated the obvious. A pilgrimage merely marked the beginning or end of a phase of your life, right? As a pilgrim, no matter how intense the discomfort, how unspeakable the boredom, you finally traipsed off whither you came—maybe changed and maybe not—back to daily life. And daily life, in our particular case, was approaching a step at a time. We walked to the railroad tracks that led, forty kilometers south, to a bus depot. Picture us three pilgrims perched on railroad tracks outside a small store drinking beer and burping that mushroom taste. I had never been so thirsty. My tongue was too swollen to taste. The beer was only a cold lump. Neither Julio nor I noticed that his nephew swilled two six-packs of beer, then gulped a half-dozen peyote segments he had stashed in his shirt pocket.

The kid in question was six feet tall, rawboned, and deferential—or he had been—but now he looked around him, crushed a beer can, and announced in a shaky voice that we were chamucos, his uncle and me, demons. He curled into a ball and wept, and then leaped to his feet. He put on quite a show. He growled and hopped and sniffed bushes and peed his pants and said Hail Marys, till both of us knew there was zero chance of getting him on the train that afternoon. When Julio suggested pushups, the fool was over three hundred and still cranking when he dropped, limp, eyes closed. By the time his breath got regular, the train was long gone. No choice but to walk to the highway and hitchhike to some hotel. Leave the kid, said Julio. He'll sleep it off and follow us into town tomorrow morning. The kid himself, the next day, said that was what I should have done. But nothing doing.

What intervened? Well, a grain of doubt, specifically my own uncertainty. Maybe the pilgrimage wasn't over. Didn't a pilgrimage let you turn a new ear for nuance to what was left of your life? For reasons I'm still figuring out, thirty years later, I shook my head. No way. And then, to the plain distaste of Julio, I shouldered the passed-out kid, and headed off in the dark toward the highway. After maybe twenty steps, the kid stiffened and hissed something about somebody's mother. Then his teeth sank into my shoulder blade. To this day, I attach a certain pride to just how far that kid flew when I launched him. He landed on cachorro thorns and blubbered and begged forgiveness. So I hoisted him, and plodded on, and he bit the very same shoulder again. Three or four exchanges like that got both of us to the highway, followed of course by Julio, barely able to walk he was laughing so hard at what he said were two very impressive—if very different—kinds of something or other.

Okay, very early the next morning, we three weary pilgrims woke in a hotel room, one I barely remembered yanking my pockets inside out the previous night to pay for. After yawning and lacing both boots, the back of my T-shirt crusty with blood, I followed a ripple of disconnection down the empty sidewalk out to the bus depot. The kid who had done the biting walked alongside, apologizing in broken Spanish, giggling, yes, but apologizing. Soon we were headed home, surrounded by grandmothers snoring, teenage mothers nursing. As daylight hit miles of huizache bush, a leaf at a time, the nuances kept building up. Neither the kid nor Julio said much when I tried to explain that double-blink headline folded on an empty seat, the one about John Lennon's murder the night before. At Charcas we caught a bus to Potosí, then to Guadalajara, from where I took a third bus back to my compadre's house.

So there you have that weekend. By now it doesn't seem so menacing. The real question maybe is why I never told anybody. There was of course the peyotero oath, so to speak, a promise to confide what happened only to another peyotero—a contract strong enough that I am only now releasing myself from it, by the way, citing the Tom Sawyer quality of the vow, even though I'm more convinced than ever that the world itself was talking to me.

Afterlife

When my bus pulls out, the big Mexican sky reflects in a puddle, and then trails nopal, rock fence, concrete telephone poles, cows, and cut banks. I'm headed to El Salto, Jalisco, to celebrate the eighty-second birthday of doña Marta, the matriarch, on the edge of Alzheimer's, of a certain family—my compadre's family—that I go back thirty-five years with. Our friendship has lasted through four divorces, the death of two fathers, and the rearing of twenty-six children; the collapse of the Mexican peso; and the relocation of six or eight million Mexicans to the United States. The stuff we re-live in each other's company! Long heartfelt talks complete with moonlight, cobblestones, and sewer odor. With a backflip of irony, when memories converge, we lead each other around terrain too raw to acknowledge. I admit it, okay, I'm headed into thirty years of shared feelings.

The feelings began in the bus depot. There I ran across Niko, my compadre's cousin, also headed to El Salto for a visit, who bought a ticket for a seat next to mine. So, in the fifteen minutes before our bus leaves, Niko knocks back three beers and dabs his eyes at how bad his luck is. He thinks he might be depressed. He comes off as a sad, lost, wandering something-or-other. He is the son of don Silvino, a difficult, cranky, demanding widower who—Niko tells me with a shrug—nowadays lives with Lola, Niko's unmarried, overachieving, gynecologist older sister who administers something like a branch clinic of El Hospital de la Mujer. Niko is headed back to celebrate Father's Day. We tilt the seats back. Conversation mode. Niko reflects that you have to credit President Fox for having controlled government spending and made it possible for banks to offer a bit of credit.

Some years ago—ten, maybe fifteen—Niko lost his job in a bank and invested his severance pay in commercial washers and driers. In his lavandería, year after year, he struggled with spiteful customers and water so filthy no filter would help, not to mention the neighbors' ill will. Finally, he moved out and bought a stall in a deserted market behind a Volkswagen dealership on Aquaducto. Now, with his machines installed, he waits days for the lights to be turned on. The thousand pesos I lend him will go for a pipa to fill his cistern.

Long divorced, Niko has one son here in town who won't speak to him, another in San Luis who manages an occasional letter, plus a daughter—from an earlier marriage—who disappeared into Texas. Niko says he's looking for a wife, someone to stay home and cook and clean, somebody glad that he comes home in the evening. His voice quivers. She doesn't have to be beautiful. That would be nice, but regular is okay. Maybe I could help Niko find somebody in el norte? A lady widowed—even divorced, who cares?—who likes to live in Mexico and has some kind of small income.

His father, Silvino, seventy-four, is a curandero by trade, in a barrio of auto repair shops and German-Shepherd-on-the-roof security, way up on a hill behind a subdivision of million-dollar homes. In a neighborhood of parabolic antennas and loose chickens, don Silvino conducts his practice from a kitchen chair, just inside the door of the corner store his wife runs. Where schoolkids traipse in for their afternoon sugar buzz, the afflicted beat a path to Silvino's chair, suffering from mal de ojo and such, from infirmities brought on by the ill will of the envious, the jealous, the spiteful.

Like the woman he treated the day I met him, a woman with an ulcerous place a foot long on her forearm. He passed his hands back and forth, palms down, an inch or so above the raw flesh, which, as he closed his eyes, began to wrinkle and sweat. It ridged; it clenched into a pattern. When his eyes snapped open, he nodded for her to study the patterns formed on her arm. She would probably see there the face of the person who paid for this to be done to her. Whereupon she recognized the features of a spiteful niece curdled right there on her own flesh. She released a pungent oath and then, over Silvino's mild protest, tucked a few bills in his shirt pocket and fled, and Silvino resumed his place on the kitchen chair.

As the bus pulls into El Salto, Niko is insisting that he tried very hard to make career connections. He tried to work his way into first one and then another of the three political parties hereabouts, even joined the Masons, but each party wanted him to work in one of the other two as a mole, passing along info. He feels off balance, you know, when he comes back like this. He feels like a gravity accident, like he wasn't built for this planet, and his father can't bear the sight of him. When the bus door opens, Niko is clenching and unclenching his fingers. Buenas noches. His voice wobbles like a pope on roller skates. He steps down. Dogs ignore him.

I wave good night and yank my suitcase uphill toward El Salto's only hotel, the Casablanca, built in Moorish style around the corner from a county building that resembles the U.S. Capitol. By eleven, I'm on the street, buying nine tacos and two Modelos, and I eat in bed, waking among the napkins around midnight when my phone rings, and Niko says he had a taxi driver deliver a Father's Day card to his father, but now he, Niko, is too nervous to answer the phone so don't call. He'll be in touch.

Most of my feelings about Mexico touch down in El Salto, forty kilometers south of Guadalajara, a town neither picturesque, nor historical, nor wealthy. It lies in Mexico's Central Highlands, and big bare hills surround it. At the far end of town, squatting under a concrete bridge, a lily-gagged pond is all that remains of the big white waterfall that gave the town its name. That waterfall, in fact, was the energy source that convinced a French millionaire to erect a textile mill, and so to found the town of El Salto, over a century ago.

Thirty years ago, the main thoroughfare was full of potholes and speed bumps, and the sidewalks tilted in all different directions. Walls used to quit mid-air at exactly the point where someone ran out of money for concrete or rebar. Even today, the plaza is nothing special: two skinny palm trees, a bandstand, and eight poured-concrete Indians forming the pillars of the bandstand. Visitors often recall them as mermaids, but no, they are Indians, and they wear bird-shit tears.

Showing up every other year, ringing the same doorbell I've been ringing for thirty years, waiting for that upstairs window to open, what I always feel, and what surprises me every time, is the sneaky pride I take in how El Salto remains part of my life. Think of the frustrated admiration you develop for a cowlick, a stammer—some unruly feature of you that thrives by resisting correction or improvement. That's El Salto.

Mi compadre, el compa, stands five foot nine, with hair gone recently white, forearms knotted from a lifetime of yanking wrenches, and skin smooth as a baby's. At sixty-five, he neither drinks nor smokes, avoids caffeine, and lives mainly on vegetables bought fresh from a cousin of his wife. He likes to talk, and to say that he is well spoken would be, shall we say, understatement in overdrive. He gets off on releasing long florid sentences from flat on his back under a pickup. As a chronicler of life in a town with a very long memory—so long that one neighbor, thirty years ago a chubby kid who liked to cinch his pants real tight, still answers to the name El Violín—el compa tells jokes that feature exotic sound effects and Siglo de Oro diction. Motor vehicles are his livelihood—buying, selling, and repairing them. When I visit, I keep him company in his shop, a cinder-block and concrete affair below his apartment, surrounded by the hoods and trunks and doors he makes a living removing dents from and then painting.

He and I met as young adults in Guadalajara, during a time of national crisis, years of kidnapping and daylight holdups and car bombs. It was an era by now not easily re-created, nor explained. I don't even recall how he and I met, but one evening, not long after we did, in the patio of the house I rented, we were enjoying the shade of a lime tree, sitting in equipales, those pigskin chairs that squeal when you shift your weight. It was warm, and the breeze carried odors of jasmine and vacant-lot garbage. Following an innocuous pause, el compa cleared his throat and asked, What do they pay you? He shook his head when I mentioned my Cultural Institute salary—no, no, no, I mean the CIA. Every leaf on that lime tree stood out for a moment. Another moment went by. Hold on, I finally managed, you've heard me talking politics, you know I'm a knee-jerk anarchist, a pop-off driven by whim and guesswork—but forget all that. Pay attention to right now: yo a mis anchas, cotorreando, y tu a chingue y chingue. You really think that some pinche CIA type would talk rascuache Spanish to you, maestro?

He squirmed; his chair creaked. He and I both knew that my last remark was nonsense. Neither one of us knew the first damn thing about CIA types. Both of us knew, as well, what everyone says about proving a negative. Plus the fact that what el compa really wanted was some excuse for believing that our friendship was on the level. Okay, he grinned. His chair squealed again. I really had to ask, you see. Because, next, I want to ask you to be godfather to my son. I told him it would be a pleasure.

In El Salto, where el compa lives, you see a familiar clash: noblesse oblige versus whatever funky survival reflex the poor count on. The town began as a brainchild of a millionaire Frenchman, one who knew state-of-the-art, nineteenth-century social engineering: barracks for single men, cottages for families, a clinic and church and school and company store, all surrounded by a twelve-foot masonry wall with a single gate. And guess who showed up to work in his mill? Those first Salteños were a hard, suspicious folk, eloquent but down-to-earth, devout and irreverent, cruel and generous—nothing like the grateful natives the Frenchman expected. By 1910, when the Mexican Revolution broke out, working folk in El Salto were so pushy they took city hall, torched the municipal archives, and sprang all the jail inmates. The streets were jammed with people yelling, ¡Borrón y cuenta nueva! Hit the reset button!

That history isn't lost on el compa. That Frenchman, when he packed up and fled—el compa will sometimes say, pausing over a fender he's painting—that Frenchman began our lengthy local tradition of flight as a way to solve problems. Cleaning one thumbnail with turpentine and a rag, he will detail local problems: bank loans come due overnight, and family businesses fold, so local boys tuck a toothbrush and a change of socks and underwear in a paper bag and make tracks. A few months go by. They manage a postcard or two, and maybe even send back money orders, but their luck runs hot and cold. Maybe once you dreamed of your viejo paying five thousand dollars to get you and the kids into el norte, but now he comes back once a year, from U.S. orchards, with all the other husbands and fathers and brothers and sons. Every January, they park shiny pickups, half on the sidewalk, both doors open, stereos wailing. El compa shakes his head. The guys walk around using a lot of English words, day and night for a month, and then drive back to those orchards. El compa bends over the fender again, squints along the paint like an archer, and nods. He wads up his rag and hands it to me, and I put it in the burn barrel.

At 9 a.m., el campa totters out of his bedroom, faltering speech, hair thin, blinking. Says he lost twenty-five kilos. Closed his repair shop and now is reduced, by the crippled economy, to bartending nights in a strip club. Meanwhile, at his elbow, curled on the sofa with her new baby, his daughter looks up without a word, and a silence washes away everything he said. She is a single mother, living with her parents, working in a factory down the road. Out of her earnings, she has paid for her mother's kitchen sink and tile floor, the windowpanes and the couch, probably the tiny washing machine that chugs on the roof.

Enter my godson and wife, her with a vinegary look, him sleek as a seal. Says he's working afternoons in a neighbor's shop with his brothers, one recently jilted, one legally separated, and one getting divorced. With just the two of us, alone over a late breakfast, my godson blurts out that he cheats on his wife, then shakes his head at how much he loves her. Once we're out on the sidewalk, he reveals that he's sleeping with the matronly mother of three, or was it four, who cleared our plates just now. But let me contextualize that remark. Life here consists of long hours at highly repetitive jobs. The tedium leaves young people scrutinizing each other like botanists. Old-growth gossip eliminates every inch of privacy.

Today's El Salto exists because of an industrial corridor running just west of it, where over three hundred labs and factories employ people from all over the country. In short, today's El Salto is a boomtown, with high-tech work for people who grew up elsewhere, while the El Salto of a generation ago was a backwater of worn-out cowboys and women abandoned by guys vanished into el norte. And yet, say what you want, the two towns feel very much alike—if only because today's Salteños moved here from towns just like El Salto, where isolation bends your thinking in favor of family and what is nearby.

El Salto is only a generation away from being a village, a place fueled by a blend of legend and gossip, where apparitions of the dead came and went as they pleased. The psychic properties of the town were startling, or would have been, if not for what was even then the crushing boredom of daily existence. For all the apparent sturdiness of patios and thick walls, of cobbled streets and a crowded graveyard, people used to overhear each other's memories. Nobody was free of what others remembered. What looked like the present flickered, and snagged, and doubled back. It is only natural, in such a town, for people to keep careful track of each other's most painful moments. Things too shameful or shameless to admit do enjoy a kind of collective-memory override. They arrive on a net of allusions and unspoken ironies, of dirty looks and airy dismissals and feigned boredom. Resentment drags at every remark.

The godson turns his ignition key, then pauses, and asks me, Do I ever write about his family?

And I gotta say yeah. Mental note: but only documentary style. Including, for example, the white malnourishment blotches on your face when you were eight, m'ijo. Including the screen-less windows and broken toilets, the single pair of shoes for a wife and two teenage boys. At first it was hard to make it believable, I start out telling him, by which I mean my own deep affection for his father, mi compa, the guy with thirteen children by three different women. Sometimes I don't believe it myself, but then what takes over is raw momentum, him and me surviving a lifetime together. Your father and I go way back, I finally say, and the godson says he knows that. He says that he himself survived by learning to keep serene, to look for good in every evil. Remember that time Jesus admired the white teeth in a putrid corpse?

At doña Marta's birthday party, her elder son—call him Omar—sits monosyllabic and perfectly straight on a sofa to one side of his mother. His brother Manolo, my compa, on her other side, has the look of a man swallowing dishwater. Clearly, the two brothers are on the outs again. Hence the abrazo they greeted each other with. Under mamá Marta's stern gaze, they hugged each other at arm's length, faces averted, jaws clenched. By now, the tension between them resembles the barely audible hum of a kitchen appliance. Maybe this is the night they trade words about who warped whose Oscar Chávez album in a backseat window thirty years before?

Anyhow, Marta absolutely glows. Visitors always make her feel alive, but it is even more delicious to sit on a sofa between grown sons, to stand and hug Felipe, their friend from, which Washington was it?

I live in the one where they grow apples, doña Marta.

And how is your family, your daughters and wife?

They are well, gracias a Dios. They send regards.

Marta looks around her. Snacks and TV fútbol are on our agenda, no? Her nod sends the two daughters-in-law off to the kitchen. Okay, maybe she doesn't entirely recognize this room, the paper flowers and caged meadow larks, tile floor and cedar beams and colonial-cut sofa, but so what? This is Marta's afternoon with the two sons that she and Candelario poured their lives into. Does Felipe know how it happened? Candelario said, after the second was born, how about we let these two boys represent us in the world? So she and Candelario never wanted more than the two.

Did you know that? Feli, did you know that we planned to have only the two children?

And that was in a time when people had many more children, verdad, doña Marta?

Un martirio, that's what it was. And the things the neighbors said!

She means that she lived in a garish, abrupt town, one where men heading downtown tucked a pistol into the back of their pants, where wives drank beer straight from the can and swore in public. Factory workers rented dance halls and bands to celebrate their children's weddings and laughed at the priest's remarks about labor unions. They were fast-talking folk with steady work who lived in company duplexes and baptized their children late, if ever. They lived for payday dice games on a blanket in an alley. Husbands disappeared on Friday afternoon and reappeared Monday morning. Behind barred windows and padlocked doors, two hard-eyed women brought in tequila and fourteen-year-old girls kidnapped from a neighboring state.

Heart surgery has left Marta so thin that her wedding band dangles. She knows she is all cheekbones and white hair. Her memory sputters like bad reception. Any talk at all is risky, so she bluffs with a smile. Or, taking the initiative, she interrupts.

Ah, forgive me. Feli, how are those two daughters of yours? And your wife?

Very well, doña Marta, thank you. They send their best wishes.

Otherwise, she utters folk sayings, terse evasions that counsel patience. Hay mas tiempo que vida, she hears herself quoting Candelario to the grandkids. After all, she's eighty-two, okay? She wants at least that much made clear. Put another way: she wants it clear that, unlike her husband, she never expected much of life. Her own low expectations somehow have been her survival kit. The payoff is this serenity which, by now, she certainly hopes that everyone observes in her.

❧　❧　❧　❧　❧

Now Omar is patting his mother's hand. On the night of her eighty-second birthday party, he announces, he has brought a truly distinguished bottle of tequila. He and Feli, his brother's compadre, go back twenty-five years, he reminds all in attendance. His voice goes skipping, one phrase to another, until it gets to the closeness of people who see each other at long intervals. He clicks glasses. We sit on the balcony, overlooking a florist, a vulcanizing shop. To us, he lifts his glass, a couple of guys getting old at the same rate.

He gives an expansive wave around him, shakes his head, and manages a tired smile. Everybody always trusted him. He trusted authority and got along. He was free of the nose-thumbing insouciance that drove his brother, right? Well, everybody was very wrong, but it took awhile to see it. He graduated in engineering and went to work for a U.S.–owned petroleum company. He married a bowlegged blonde with a laugh like a pneumatic wrench, and they promptly had four children. Installing his family among wide yards, electric-door garages, and picture windows, he felt grateful, but a little cheated. He felt like he had no friends. One night he got so drunk he peed his pants at a stoplight.

Never mind what happened next. His mother wound up telling the neighbors that he lost his heart to a younger woman, a woman he met at work, the daughter of a professional baseball player, no less. The two of them rented a house in a working-class neighborhood. Four more children were born. Pretty quickly, of the four kids from his first marriage, only the oldest boy, the namesake, would so much as speak to him. The namesake decided to study engineering like his dad and even came by on Sundays to take his half brothers and sisters to the zoo. After a tense pause, Omar begins choosing his words: I don't recall when it was that he started losing weight. Before long, he looked like his face would break when he smiled.

Omar refills the glasses and cuts another lime. We were desperate. One diagnosis after another fell apart. By the time I found an internist— some chilanguito, second-generation Lebanese—and the guy realized that he was looking at a heart infection, my kid was in intensive care, barely able to suck on a drinking straw. Anyhow, only a week later, the good doctor Cuatehmoc Bey, he asked me, he asked me seventeen times in a row, did I want him to jump-start that hairless chest again. After I said to let him go, I shut that hospital door, and set out to be the Catholic that I always should have been. I plain wore out the hospital grief counselors, then the parish priest. I tried everything, Omar says. When he made a pilgrimage to Talpa, he says, he woke every morning full of a limping, grudging wonder.

Omar's own survival astounded him. It was like being unpleasantly surprised. Right away, he got very stingy with time, checking his e-mail four times a day, installing an egg timer by the phone to limit his calls to three minutes. The more he got used to being alive, the more he slowed down, examined, measured. He bought light-sensitive bifocals, and then tramped out to archaeological zones nearby. He haunted state museums and bent over the pottery figures yielded by the region's very oldest tombs: small men and women caught in energetic poses, some in exaggerated expressions of fear or delight, others introspective, reserved. Some wore intricately folded loincloths, with rattles and fans in hand, and removable headdresses, while others had bodies rounded or flattened. Soon he was squinting at titles in flea markets. Now his bookshelves groan with volumes of ancient western Mexico's archaeology.

Western Mexico is mainly mile-high lake beds, an eerie place where dust devils flit each spring and the ground sags with rain and corn by summer. You find no pyramids or limestone highways here because local people, two millennia ago, apparently rejected that ugly rigamarole of human heart and hummingbird, the jade-skirt-and-obsidian-mirror routine. But local folk knew what worship was. Omar figures they were proto-healers, nameless people who flew or descended through air or earth and opted, in the end, for no pyramid at all.

When it was time to die, he figures, they stretched out in shaft-and-chamber tombs and called it even. Believing that lets him fall asleep with a young wife snoring beside him on Sunday night. And it helps him hit the road on Monday morning, all aftershave and laptop, Day Runner, cell phone. He wears starched and ironed coveralls and his boots gleam. Heel-taps, no less. When Omar walks down the sidewalk, it sounds like cellophane unwrapping.

꒰   ꒰   ꒰   ꒰   ꒰

Raquel, Omar's second wife, is the daughter of a professional baseball player, a fellow long on drink and short on words. He had huge forearms, tiny feet, and squint wrinkles. After he felt his arm twinge and quit one afternoon in a near-empty stadium in Aguascalientes, he acquired a wife the way someone else would acquire a hotel-lobby shoe shine. The nine kids that followed let him joke that he could field a team. Raquel remembers the paint-peeling apartments where Mother cooked on a hot plate. She remembers Mexican League baseball, one desert town to another, the old man asleep on the couch with a beer in his hand, and a game on that tiny black-and-white TV. He tucked the TV away alongside his spikes and glove and the hot plate in the trunk and waved everybody aboard.

The day her older brother died, aged twenty—well, es de, Raquel never knows if talking about it will make her feel better or worse. She was prowling the grandstand selling soda pop, and the fastball that hit him in the throat made a sound like your palm against masa. She felt her hand go numb around the plastic bottle of Fanta she was extending to a fat man in a John Lennon T-shirt. From a long way off, she heard her father's voice scolding her brother to get up. She watched her father prod him a couple of times with a bat and turn away. That night, he told the family never again to mention the boy's name in his presence. And he himself never uttered the name until twenty years later, thrashing with cirrhosis in a charity ward, he began yelling it. After she changed his diaper, she wet his lips so he could keep apologizing.

Marta has a dreamy look on her face. Sixty-five years ago today, Candelario told her—on the day she turned seventeen, family legend has it—that if she didn't marry him he'd carry her off that very night, so that nobody else would want her. Except that Marta isn't entirely sure it happened that way. Frankly, it sounds made up. From this end of her life, she can't always separate what she lived through from what is merely good storytelling. Nowadays, after all, in the shade of what is left of the Frenchman's masonry wall, people her age occupy benches and recall when Cinco de Mayo Street finally penetrated the Frenchman's stronghold. The street promptly collected pool halls and taco stands, and ever since then living in El Salto has injected a certain fervor into your life.

The storytelling feature of Marta's life began to take over on that morning her younger son closed a bedroom door behind him and told her she was a widow. She remembered sitting alone at the kitchen table to think. Her husband had been wrong, she decided. Dignity was appearing to want whatever it was that someone stronger wanted you to want. And so she began by forgetting her pills, her grandchildren's birthdays. Then a kettle boiled dry on her stove. She wound up in a vegetable market, bag in hand, dabbing her eyes and shaking her head. How is she supposed to feel? Everybody looks at the floor.

Paula, Manolo's second wife, hands Marta a tissue. Paula is a borderline character in this family narrative and knows it. Paula is tall and wide and fair of skin, which is why Manolo picked her out, though she, by God, knew from the start that her in-laws thought she was a rube, una correntona. At first, she felt completely alone at night in a roomful of open-mouthed people with their eyes trained on what they figured was the outside world in the form of TV screens. She was way too self-conscious. She grew up across the bridge, way on the other side of a river now choked with lilies nourished by waste from the denim factory. Every Tuesday night the factory released an odor like baby shit.

Paula's feelings radiate like tree rings. It is hard to find where any one of them starts. It gives her an absent-mindedness which her in-laws take for brooding. She's lonely when they gather. She never disagrees. When she feels a tingle like her toes are disappearing, she will nod or repeat the last words of what you said. Or even flip her eyes and palms skyward in emphatic agreement. To express the deepest dimensions of agreement, she responds with a four- or five-sentence tale, in a child-like pitch, about some occurrence that took place right here, or only a block away, one hundred years ago.

She has the fair skin and blue eyes and reddish hair that incursions of French and German folk a century and a half ago deposited in the Central Highlands. But her speech is full of terms that date from digging-stick times. Taimada, her mother-in-law calls her, alluding to the absorbent impassivity of peasants. Paula is taciturn and monosyllabic, which leaves her in-laws observing that she is either shy or sly, depending on whether the observer also notices that she nearly always gets her way. Those blue eyes fix on the middle distance, her jaw sets, and things happen.

჻ ჻ ჻ ჻ ჻

To understand my compa Manolo, start with his love life. For motives he himself has never understood—who is he to understand?—Manolo has always attracted women. He has charmed them standing or sitting, on folding chairs and church pews, in hammocks and on banisters, in water both salt and fresh, on picnic tables and swing sets, in steam rooms and movie theaters and opera boxes, once in a sleeping bag at 11,000 feet, a couple of times on horseback, and no, make that twice in the sleeping bag. The very day he turned thirteen, a motel maid stood with her knuckles in suds and her skirt around her waist and came and wept and promised to be his forever. Okay, maybe the banker's wife

from the weekend before last wasn't really in love with him. But thinking that she was, well, it certainly beat recalling her as a skinny repelona
with sour breath who made a guy shower and use a condom.

Love itself, you could say, drove el compa from el norte. His first
and only venture north had started with an unexpected blessing from
his father. It wasn't worth remembering what they said, they hadn't
spoken for weeks, but the gesture was eloquent. On a stretch of asphalt
and roadkill, embracing him in front of strangers, the old man was
acknowledging, but not endorsing, the way of life his son was choosing,
so very different from his own. The son managed six months survival
up north, part-time, piecework, sleeping on friends' couches.

El compa wound up bent over an examining table, pants at his
ankles, somebody rubber-gloving that prostate infection he figured later
he must've picked up from a long-haired teenager who wore no underwear and introduced him to mint oil. Or maybe the Columbia Basin
hussy who drove him out to her trailer, where he woke up naked beside
her under a bedsheet when her kids' a.m. TV cartoons arrived full blast
at the foot of the bed, and he jackknifed awake with one long ¡híííjole!
and clutched the sheet, and she scolded him not to swear in front of her
children. One of those two.

Although even then he was secretly grateful to the prostate infection that sent him back—on the very next plane—to live the rest of his
days in a country where there was time for stuff. Time for two elderly
men to step over a dead dog in the street, never noticing, they're so busy
greeting each other. That kind of time was what his father lived in. After
a guy had sired a certain number of kids, and owed a certain amount
of money, one last bit of willpower might get triggered by no more
than sunlight outlining the thigh of the vegetable vendor's daughter. His
father had reared him to work hard, Manolo told himself, to expect
only the right to keep some corner of himself off limits.

❧ ❧ ❧ ❧ ❧

Don Chino lived his whole life, as they say, a la antigua, at the pace of
a former age. He was a bus driver, tall and slender and reserved, with
manners so quaint and graceful they brought out good manners in other
people. You never saw him in a hurry. He poured a mean shot of rum
and posed thoughtful questions about U.S. geography. The occasional
classical allusion textured his speech, as when he said once that his life,

which had begun with the century, by now resembled that of Sisyphus. He had grown up poor, in a village five hours away.

He rode a stagecoach into Guadalajara at age fifteen to seek his fortune. On arrival, he washed his face and spent his next-to-last centavos on a pocket comb, then set out hunting work. He worked like hell, becoming yard boy to a university rector, and even beginning the study of medicine. But after five years, when the governor replaced the rector, Chino had to start driving a bus. When it became clear that life had no intention of treating him kindly—that was when he started quoting Marcus Aurelius to himself. If what ailed you had a cure, what was the problem? And if it had no cure, what was the problem? Or was that Epictetus, Chino winked. He wasn't above amusing himself with the visiting schoolteacher.

Imagine the young Chino, picking out his bride, a fifteen-year-old with high cheekbones, huge eyes, and a silky voice. Her name was Marta. Family legend has him carrying her off—se la llevó, in the fashion of the day—because who would marry a girl that spent a night with a guy, whether she went willingly or not? The marriage that resulted lasted more than fifty years. It survived what historians call the Modernization of Mexico, which dislocated several million sharecropper families into urban apartments and alleys and vacant lots to work as albañiles and criadas: housekeeping and grunt labor. By the time the marriage ended, both partners tottered, exhaust fumes wrinkled their view out the window, and plants shriveled on the patio.

Ten or twelve years into the marriage, Chino pulled into the bus station one afternoon. A young lady he was seeing occupied the seat behind his own, and Marta waited on the sidewalk, fists on her hips. A crowd gathered when Marta and the girlfriend squared off. In a silence so thick you could hear the curb splat a skull, you heard a gasp, a sigh. On a driveway crunchy with bottle caps and candy wrappers, cigarette butts and spit, those two women rolled back and forth. It seemed to take forever. Marta stood up, finally, and the other woman didn't. Marta wore a split lip and was missing a patch of hair. She put one arm around Chino, the other around the two little boys in school uniforms standing there openmouthed, and the family went up to dinner.

૩   ૩   ૩   ૩   ૩

One November, many years later, Manolo shook my hand, then shut off the compressor, and sat on the steps. A tired, pre-recorded voice came out of him. It took a moment to catch on. He was saying that his father was dead. El jefe died right here at home, entiendes? Shut himself in the back bedroom, wouldn't let in anybody but me.

He wouldn't check into a hospital?

Pos', you know how he was. He was don Chino. Couldn't go anywhere smelling like that. It was humiliating. Whatever it was that killed him—he never wanted to know what it was—had him fouling one mattress after another. I never smelled anything like it. But get this. I got to where I could eat lunch sitting at the foot of his bed.

He didn't want to know what he had?

Wasn't at all interested. At the end, when his lungs filled up, he pretended not to notice. The only concession he made, when his breathing slowed down, was he said he would gladly live another ninety years, but only in a body made of stuff less perishable, and what was there to say after that?

A long moment went by. Busses went whining through the streets, and a bell tower was clanging away, and a roof-top dog was barking. It felt like when you can't think of a word. Finally, Manolo exhaled and started scrubbing his knuckles in a bucket. After all, don Chino had reared his boys to believe that self-control was the mother of dignity.

≈   ≈   ≈   ≈   ≈

One time at the edge of a street in El Salto, a couple of guys were killing time with a pellet rifle. Yawning and scratching and stretching, they were shooting at a small lizard halfway up the adobe wall across the street. Ping, one of them let fly at the lizard. They nodded buenos días to the by then middle-aged don Chino as he walked by with a plastic bag of pop bottles. Chino nodded and, without a word, without even breaking stride, pulled out a bottle and held it at arm's length as he trudged uphill. Ping. Ping, ping. People remembered little touches of generosity like that.

Chino saw big changes in the town. In time, the labor movement took over city hall, and vice versa. Which is to say that once both the movement and city hall were freed of reforming dissidents—by a pound of parking-lot dynamite one afternoon, no less—the same families held office, and the years went by in slow motion. You'd have thought that the names of local boys Pelón Gutiérrez and Chino Ozorno would live forever, from the way that drunks carried on at factory fútbol games. Every visit from a party candidate called for floral arches, schoolkid choirs, and mariachi bands. Once, they said, a line of black sedans with the presidential seal had to wait at one edge of town while presidential security frisked the mayor. Only with His Honor installed in plain sight at the right hand of the president of the republic could the caravan pass through town.

What is for sure is that, at age fifteen, Chino rode a stagecoach from his village in the sierra to Guadalajara. Under a rainy late-spring sky, young Candelario counted the canyons until he saw the gray spire and iron railings of Guadalajara. It was going to be his town. But the moment he slicked back his hair, eighty years flew by, and he lay on a mattress that reeked, and fluids leaked out when he slept or lost his concentration. He banned his wife and the older boy from the room. He kept the younger boy by his bed to fetch sips of water and the morning paper. He hadn't the least idea what was killing him, nor did he ask. After driving a bus for fifty of his eighty-some years, weaving the same route between tequila factories and opal mines, he died bidding so long to the wife and the older boy through a bedroom door, no offense. It was his way of getting the last word in.

Like a guy taking a squeegee to a penthouse windowpane, that is how Chino feels by now. Even though he himself by now amounts to little more than an atmosphere that clings to words and wallpaper, notice that—after sixty-five years of silence and shrugs and quotes from the Latin he learned in his altar-boy days and never forgot—Chino has pulled off a tiny miracle, depositing enough of himself that his wife and sons for a moment imagine him in place at the head of the table the night of Marta's eighty-second birthday. Although, Chino wants to add, it is merely a trick of willpower, predictable the minute you see it, and like this whole afterlife business, something of a letdown.

꒦꓃   ꒦꓃   ꒦꓃   ꒦꓃   ꒦꓃

The next morning, on the way out of town, I stopped at the clinic to see Niko's sister Lola, not that she and I are especially close, but after my lengthy bus ride with her brother, I wanted to say hello at least, and ask after her father, and take a look at the clinic. But I arrived at an awkward moment. She was beginning the very first in a series of community health seminars. She spotted me in the doorway, grinned, looped the lanyard of a little camera around my wrist, and begged me to take photos.

Imagine 250 plastic chairs in rows in a meeting room, and it is hot, with a couple of hundred Sras. fanning their faces with pamphlets for the VpH test Lola by now is describing on the blackboard in front of them. Twenty fotos taped to the wall show the process of inserting the stick with soft bristles up to the end of the vagina, twisting five times—but not like you're stirring soup, says Lola—then extracting and placing the stick in a small plastic bottle, breaking off the stick, sealing the bottle. Results available the last Thursday of the month.

From the back of the room, I notice too late that the only door is at the front—to exit now would draw attention—and so I figure well, okay, ready-aim-fire. Which button did she say to push? Point blank. Secretaries from municipal offices in velour pantsuits, designer jeans, wedge sandals and high heels, a couple of leather jackets, gotcha. Three women from the Integral Family Development office sit at the table in front taking data while each Sra. disappears into the john. As Lola demonstrates, in Levi's and polo shirt, how to separate your legs and half crouch, warning again and again that the kits cost one thousand pesos each, I start to get less self-conscious. How many shots did she say to take? Five of the nearest Sras. wear barrettes of leather, rhinestones, elastic, each in earrings and eye shadow. Late arrivals smile in polyester blouses and hoop earrings and perfume. A fan-purr in one corner; plastic chairs and Formica conference tables; tile floors; chipped white, sliding plastic-frame windows; screens and vertical blinds.

On a hunch I save the last two exposures, thank God, because when Lola launches into her third rendition of "you drop your trousers and then your undies and only an inch of brush sticks out," emphasizing that Pfizer put up $20,000 for materials and that the PANista presidente municipal came up with funds for expenses, right then, as they say as if on cue, the municipal first lady appears, silk blouse and tailored slacks, umbrella and shades and pearl earrings, and awards Lola a campaign-style peck on the cheek.

Pre-dawn ride. The airport. Handshake with Beto the taxista. I lurch up a ramp past a skycap asleep on his dolly. All is okay at the ticket desk until the airline agent wants my exit visa, looks, and shakes her head no, sorry. I get sent upstairs to a darkened office, and knock, and wake a guy stretched on a couch, who rubs his eyes and motions me to a back room. I sit. He tells me I can't leave the country—no exit visa—and gotta go back to Inmigración and ask for a temporary. Back at the ticket desk, the same poor agent keeps piping her grade-school English at me, favoring me with a smile that she must hope will turn my malice into resignation, but doesn't.

The next day, when I return with the paperwork—somehow I thought that Inmigración would mail it to me—she smiles and says, You're back, to which I say, Sí, probando suerte—trying my luck again—at which we both laugh. Finally I'm off into a wispy sky, yawns all around me. I look out the window: goodbye to the United Mexican States, a country cruel and puzzling and sweet, with a memory longer than God's.

The landing gear drops, and I'm in the Houston airport, knapsack and computer bag in one hand, in the other the plastic bag—thirty pounds at least—which the elderly Sra. beside me was staggering under. Her ankle hurts—diabetes, she says. The two of us set out hiking through one hall after another. She's from Chihuahua, she says, and where am I from? Well, I start in, it depends. But when a uniformed INS agent—accent from Pakistan? from India?—scolds the Sra. and me into line, right then, I wanna scream at the fool, Hold on! You can't talk to us like that! Not right here, not in our own goddam, hmm, well, anyway.

In half an hour I'm on another plane, pressed against a window. My seat mates are a three-hundred-pound mother with a chubby tot and a guy passed out with the *Book of the Dead* in his lap. Not one empty seat on the plane. The Oklahoma-sounding captain announces a flat tam of three r's and fitty-nine minnits. The kid, teething, drools and howls. Deep breath, deep breath. Border-drag, let us call it, a huge, invisible resistance. Finally, a landing gear drops at Sea-Tac Airport, and the pretty woman I am married to strolls up. I give her my Humphrey Bogart monkey-shit sidewinder once-over. And she falls for it. I can tell.

Carlos and Pera Were Lovers

One Saturday afternoon, in a corner at the food bank, while a dozen families lined up, nodding hello and talking about the snow-flurried roads that led east across the river into winter sagebrush, where clutches of trailers huddled, Pera and Carlos bagged masa. Scraps of onion skin scattered on the floor. A limp cardboard box that once held frozen turkey quarters lay underfoot; Carlos and Pera were trying very hard to find something to talk about. Scoop and tie, scoop and tie. When their knuckles brushed, and a fine white cloud formed over the mouth of the sack, they sneezed and grinned.

Did she come from Guerrero?

Acapulco, yes.

He thought so because of her accent.

Oh, a smile, and where was he from?

He cleared his throat and looked her in the eye. He tried to think of something unforgettable. He was the love child, he wanted to say, of a runaway jipiteca taken in by a childless Kíkapu couple living under the Piedras Negras bridge. All of that with a straight face. But no, all he said was, from Michoacán. She took a long look at him. The guy had possibilities. When he broke out in a grin, she smiled and looked away, but only for the moment it took to reply that she was happy to make his acquaintance, etc.

Then Carlos wondered, very cautiously, would she like to go window shopping downtown, sure, and after that they went for coffee in a MacDonald's. They sat against a window overlooking large plastic tubes kids slid through and came out of howling. They talked about the food bank, about jobs, about stuff she couldn't recall a moment later because it felt so good that someone was asking her questions and nodding at what she said. Her own thoughts leaping clear, wiggling off in she didn't care what direction. Watch out, she told herself that night. She repeated his name and told herself to watch out for those large calm eyes. He made her think of somebody steering through fog. He made her think of telenovelas written to draw in people like Carlos and her, even if the characters in them were stereotypes of Carlos and her. It wasn't that you identified with the singsong housemaid in braids, after all, especially not when she was pregnant by her employer's smooth-talking brother-in-law, but the hassle she went through did sound familiar. And for that matter, so did the brother-in-law.

The first lovemaking Pera and Carlos enjoyed was certainly nothing out of a telenovela. They got it out of the way in almost business-like fashion one afternoon in her aunt's trailer before the nieces got home from school. Pera had just got back from the supermarket when Carlos came by and helped carry in the grocery bags, and one thing led to another, not so much out of passion as because it was what people did, this curious, sweaty, grinding, clumsy dance that left them with nothing to say, kind of embarrassed, but closer, she knew, to each other than before. Their love affair made quite a hit with the neighbors, it turned out, as Pera in her hurry to get indoors had left the headlights on, so in a couple of hours, when Carlos came out, he had to borrow jumper cables from the grinning guy next door, and, well, so much for discretion.

There never was a public or ceremonial moment to celebrate what now existed between Pera and Carlos. Though the family acknowledged it in ways as inconspicuous as rearranging the contents of her aunt's crowded medicine cabinet to include Carlos's toothbrush and razor, and the sleeping arrangements became fluid, with one of the twins spending nights with a cousin across the street, and the other announcing she needed to sleep on the living room couch because she was studying late.

That was how the lovers settled into the bedroom that Pera not long before had shared with the twins. For each, it was a relatively stable routine of working, sleeping, and small talk, though anyone less used to impermanence would have felt it truly chaotic. Neither had a steady job nor a place to live. But neither was quite ready to let go of a certain independence, the rush that came with wholesale imperma-nence, the guilty relief there was in all this loneliness. Neither at the moment could have fallen, so to speak, in love. Not with a person's whole life blinking off and on, no thanks. Instead, with mixed feelings, they eased into each other.

The relationship acquired a wary guardedness. They trusted each other, and they didn't. Soon, they barely spoke. What was there to talk about? They shared the same floor space, but when they shared sex in the dark, without a word, half-embarrassed, it was nearly anonymous, which was how each preferred it. Longer-lasting feelings they shared, if at all, with intimates of their own gender, siblings, cousins, even in-laws. Neither was going to give up a certain hard-won privacy, and neither did. So their marriage—never solemnicized as such until the oldest child was ten—became an afterthought. Their lives, very likely, would've bored anybody but people exactly like them. Neither expected very much.

Carlos, to begin with, kept his socks and underwear in the nylon bag he brought with him, that and two hangers of clothing, a jacket, a pair of boots. And she began by not trying too hard, no probing questions, alert, sparrow-at-the-window style, no telling how long. After a few days, the least degree of curiosity trickled into his tone. He laughed at something she said. One morning she woke to find his pants hung over a chair and his pocket knife and loose change on the table beside their bed—which was now indeed their bed.

What happened was that Carlos made a decision. He would act content, but be ready to flee at the least hint of you-know-what. It wasn't that he wanted to leave. But she better act like he was free to leave. Otherwise, he couldn't bear the look that went across other guys' faces at the sight of him. Freedom was the #1 rule of love itself, that sublime foxpaw. Created by a couple of the gods for reasons they promptly forgot. Nonetheless, if you happened to look through the Laundromat window and caught sight of Carlos, standing there with cling-free fabric softener in one hand and a wad of plain white cotton undies and bras in the other, studying the dial on a dryer, well, you kept right on walking.

It was at the food bank where they met people from places they had barely heard of: Durango, Veracruz, Tamaulipas. They took turns out front, perched on a plastic chair, writing down names like Eleuterio and Plutarco, Baltazar and Epigmenio. One by one. Number of family members. State of origin. Every single one of these people had fingerprints engineered by the angel of specificity. But otherwise all they shared was endless optimism. The Israelites released from Egypt—emitting full-throated hosannas and generally putting on the dog—hadn't as sharp a sense of la tierra prometida as immigrant Mexicans did.

One afternoon, while Pera was sacking masa with Chole, her aunt, an elderly woman went by balanced—with apparent glee—on the handlebars of a bicycle. The bike was pedaled by a teenage guy with a stoic look. Pera nodded after them. ¿La Sra. quién es?

Bueno, Aunt Chole began. She sat down and collected her thoughts. Pues, la mentada 'ñora se puso a discutir con el mozo aquel ciertos aspectos de lo que es el amor verdadero, sabes. Said little old lady was one day discussing—who knows why?—the nature of true love with her houseboy, that young man right there. And when the 'ñora declared that she herself was still a virgin, the kid apparently laughed in her face.

Really? The kid laughed?

A carcajadas, el carajo, Chole scowled. Then Chole sniffed and said something about stubborn country people. About their forever putting things in the form of a wager, ella que sí, el que ni madres. Anyhow, the end of the tale was simplicity itself. The two of them went to bed, and the 'ñora won the bet, whereupon they got married, and now she rode into town perched on his handlebar.

¡Válgame! said Pera.

Chole nodded and crossed herself. Hijo, estás allá? Chole turned and shouted through the doorway into a dark room where the Salazar sisters, matching socks, grinned with satisfaction when the kid at their feet, under the table, responded, Sí, estoy allá.

Every other Wednesday, Vinnie Maltese the truck driver pulled in, scruffy and raffish and from New Jersey. Irish mother and Italian father. He wore a goatee; his hair was dyed blond. All week long he delivered pallets of rice and beans, produce and canned fruit, and boxes of blankets and winter coats to food banks in three counties. Weekends, he played drums at the Eagles Lodge—Yakima, Prosser, Sunnyside—with Nervous Brian the guitarist. Vinnie always climbed out of his cab practicing the phrase buenos días. Vinnie liked to shoot the shit. My folks talked Italian at the dinner table. They didn't want the kids to learn it. Buncha guys like us playin' grab-ass in the park, we better be American. So when Grandma Maltese's cat got run over by a bus—she was over eighty at the time—and she cut loose in Italian from a second-story window, a teenage cousin closed the window. English, Grandma. This is America.

Labor Day weekend approached, featuring the local rodeo, an event hyped so endlessly by the local newspaper and Chamber of Commerce that anticipation spread at last into mexicano households. Schoolkids began bringing home handbills, and people took special notice of Captain America, a traveling daredevil with a press release stating that he would dive from a 110-foot tower into a water tank 3 feet deep. Ensuing press releases varied the height of the tower, the depth of the water, at one point even adding rattlesnakes to the tank, all of which raised eyebrows. What kind of people would pay to see something like that? The Captain's daily risk adjustment, as reported umpteenth hand, had become a standing joke between Pera and Carlos. Allusions to swimming rattlesnakes and gullible gabos made for a pleasure they shared with no one else, an irony beam they directed at where they lived.

Carlos bought Saturday tickets. And Saturday afternoon they walked downtown at noon, through sidewalks thronged with parade watchers. The parade included five antique fire engines, one U.S. senator, three honorary sheriff posses, two high school marching bands, the queen and her court, an antique thresher pulled by horses, and three teenagers sweeping up after the horses. Pera and Carlos told each other they wouldn't have missed it for the world. It was a chance to see accountants from Bellevue in Stetsons and snakeskin boots sharing a moment and a beer with mexicano ranch hands in baseball caps and shower sandals.

They passed under a big wooden beam, into a low stadium with canopied seating and a dirt arena. And in the passageway, for the first time in their lives, the two of them were surrounded completely by white people, the smell and bulk of white people, those huge pale arms and legs, wispy hair, pink scalp. The way everybody stiffened, squirmed, averted their eyes, it made you miss the squishy feel of a Guadalajara rush-hour bus. Pera and Carlos found their seats by him taking her arm in a way that left no doubt she was with him, though he kept hoping her feelings were as mixed as his own. She sat down, and her eyes narrowed. She dug her fingernails into her palm, wondering how long this was going to be. As to what happened out there in that arena, neither Pera nor Carlos understood much of it. They soon forgot the whole thing. They were still several years from acquiring the innocence and wariness and gullibility necessary to sit there watching strangers get launched off the backs of horses and bulls. They watched guys in clown suits. Finally, they saw Captain America himself, a little fat guy with a dab of black mustache. He wore pinstriped warm-up pants—red, white, and blue. He wore a T-shirt that was stenciled, on the front, Anybody Born in Missouri, and then on the back, Is Bound to See Trouble.

The Captain jumped off a ten-foot cherry picker into a chicken-wire corral one hundred feet across and leaped to his feet karate style to face a couple of fleeing rattlers, each about four inches long. Rodeo assistants whisked his props away and nabbed the snakes with a dogcatcher's pole. They dropped them into plastic garbage cans. Then Pera and Carlos went home, and the wild-cow milking started up, with everybody cheering for their brother-in-law or cousin out there cutting capers in the dung and the dust.

≥   ≥   ≥

The Expatriation of Miguel Sevilla Oñates, aka El Pájaro

Because he practiced English day and night, he was ready the morning the state university called. They needed someone to interpret for an investigator, a certain doctora in her fifties—khaki shorts, briefcase, sandals— who went around asking questions about the local diet. She had a grant to study it. That much he knew from a sister-in-law who hosted this lady for two nights on a cot. La Doctora never complained, his sister-in-law said. In a knapsack, she carried a toothbrush and mosquito netting. She ate trail mix and bathed, as she could, under a driveway faucet.

El Pájaro and La Doctora were on an ejido an hour outside Morelia, in the kitchen of another one of his aunts, at a table with four Sras. Rain hammered the corrugated metal roof, a naked lightbulb dangled, and in the center of the table sat a jar of Nescafé and a sugar bowl. It got so quiet you could hear the guzzling where a new mother stood with a towel draped over the infant she held at port arms. Kindling crackled under the stove lid. A rafter creaked.

From the beginning, he thought of La Doctora as his ticket to el norte. She was an escape route from the small-town life he was sure was going to suffocate him. He'd had it with gossipy neighbors, pothole streets, and the same bedraggled parades every year passing the same spray-painted statues. He was desperate. He hated everything about his hometown—beginning with the nickname it stuck on him one afternoon when the family dog, up on the roof, went into convulsions from what they figured was poison. So young Miguel was sent up to seize the dog's tail and spin the dog until it got dizzy and vomited, except that he got dizzy first and fell off the roof and broke his arm, and after that people called him El Pájaro, "the Bird."

One by one now, prompting each other, the women at the table were recollecting the week's meals. Behind them stood another dozen señoras, wary, watchful.

Quelites, responded the elderly señora at the table. She waved away her momentary forgetfulness—one finger was missing two joints—and hissed for emphasis, Quelites.

The investigator looked at El Pájaro, who thought and shook his head. He looked unprepared, and he knew it. He wished he had the dictionary he'd left behind, the one he didn't want to look like he needed. Well, he frowned, it's like when you pick plants, you make a salad.

Greens, she nodded, producing a yellow pencil. She checked a column in a notebook.

Ask what she ate with her salad.

¿Qué más comió? he said, and shrugged at the quizzical look the elderly woman gave him.

Salad only, he said.

Ask if the family consumes dairy products, please.

¿Comen Uds. productos lacteos?

¿Productos . . .?

¿La leche, por ejemplo, el queso?

Cosa muy eventual, Sr.

Rarely, she says.

The pencil didn't move, so El Pájaro pressed for more detail. ¿Cada cuándo?

Pos' sabrá Dios, desde que la vaca se metió en la carretera, que se nos extravió.

¿Y?

Pos' la plancharon bien y bonito.

Not since their cow got run over, El Pájaro deadpanned. The investigator shot him a look over her notebook—a smile or a bit of indigestion?

Then the rain got so loud he had to read lips to interpret. Then it veered off so fast it left him shouting what someone had for lunch the day before. Crowded into a corner, he couldn't lift his hand to see his wristwatch, but judged it must be after four. The Sras. took their time. They were very thorough.

The last informant, a tiny, wrinkled grandmother, went absolutely speechless at her daughter's suggestion that she, the week before, had consumed a pork chop at a wedding. Que soy aventista—she reminded all present that her Adventist faith boasted rigid dietary restrictions—y no comemos de eso. En absoluto.

Amá, por favor, a middle-aged woman broke in. Somos puros católicos, she addressed the investigator, en primer lugar, y en segundo, le encantan los chicharrones.

Now was the moment to press the limits, El Pájaro figured. The family's been Catholic since Cortés, he translated, and the 'ñora lives on pork rinds.

The investigator hid a grin, but the woman, as if she understood every word, drew herself upright, and held out uplifted hands. Exactly what was her daughter's testimony worth? Especially compared to one's own powers of recall, which went back to when don Lázaro, president of the republic, appeared in this very town and stood in her doorway and asked for lunch.

El Pájaro, on the way out of town, had to wonder how the president ever found the place. He himself hadn't been here in ten years, and so on the way out of town, his directions took them the long way around, past the schoolhouse—scratchy blackboards, crumbling chalk, bronze plaque—past a rusted-out sedan, over a slick red road gushing with gaps and cracks, a road shoulder that vanished into weeds. Finally, the gravel road that led to the highway that led to Morelia. But La Doctora seemed not to mind. You must have studied English many years, she said.

When she looked at him, his mind took off. Her look brought back the peculiar wiggle he felt one afternoon in a Mexico City department store, eleventh floor, perfume counter, a look he shared with a salesclerk while bottles tilted, tipped, glittered, and settled again, a look unbearably intimate. The clerk was maybe twenty, thin legs, bad haircut. As neither of them could think what to say right afterwards, he grinned and shook her hand and left.

It took an instant to reply. No, I just visit family in el norte a lot.

Let the idea dangle, he told himself, undeveloped. Master of elastic detail that he was, he could wring any number of special effects from what were, in truth, a couple of summers picking California fields with Cousin Beto, never out of sight of the border. She shifted her gaze from the windshield to him and back. Interested, no? She was so close it was hard to breathe.

Do you know the Yakima Valley? She pulled up to a stoplight.

More less, yes.

He wagged a finger at a guy who approached, limping, with rag in hand. No, compa, gracias. The guy swerved to the driver's side of the windshield, aimed a squirt bottle, and got off a round before El Pájaro tensed and hissed, Déjelo, sinvergüenza. The guy with the spray leaned forward, studied El Pájaro through the windshield, and walked to the car behind them, leaving a blur the size of a human head for La Doctora to look through. The light turned green, and they went through the intersection. This people, El Pájaro said, and rolled his eyes. He fought an urge to look back, but felt something different in himself: never before had he felt so much disdain and shame about where he was from. His hands shook. He wanted to disappear.

At the airport, she glided from behind the wheel, around a row of parked cars, producing a credit card at the rental desk. She turned to him with a heart-thud smile, handshake firm and prolonged. She put in his hand a business card, fumbling the only Spanish she had spoken all afternoon. Allí tienes tu casa, a traditional Mexican invitation. Thanks, she said again and was gone. The card held a logo, and below it said she was director of the Cascade Food Bank. ¡Órale! Right then and there, pro forma invite that it was, El Pájaro decided to believe he would be welcome—more than welcome—to visit the lady. On a warm autumn night, at what he hoped was the beginning of his life—the real beginning—it felt like the right thing to believe.

☙　☙　☙　☙　☙

Ten days later, it still did. Now, three thousand miles north, La Doctora did a double take in the four strides it took her to reach him and extend her hand to El Pájaro. And right there, he shed illusions, in roughly equal proportions, about 1) her interest in him, and 2) his own future in el norte. Plans evaporating. This time he really wanted to disappear. La Doctora was a very plain, middle-aged, schoolteacher-looking woman with dull brown hair and a crooked nose. She cleared her throat.

I'm sorry, your name?

Miguel Sevilla Oñates, a sus órdenes, he purred. You remember me?

The same smile that he read, in the car, as a come-on might indicate, he now saw, neither invitation nor indigestion, but only annoyance, barely controlled. He took a step backward. She wasn't the same person. She wore glasses here, one earpiece held with a paper clip, and here she was in charge. Here, in the flat light that overhead fixtures threw on cardboard boxes and sacks of masa, she was in charge. He was a fool, he told himself. He was exactly the same kind of ridiculous fraud that windshield-wiping cripple was. He felt a surge of energy. He took a step forward, hands crossed behind his back, and opened his mouth to apologize. But La Doctora interrupted.

I bet we can find you a place to stay, Miguel. Just like that, La Doctora said it, after a moment adding, We even can find work for you here in the food bank until you get a job.

He was floored, dazed. He suddenly felt an urge to make some provocative remark, to draw her into asking why he was here. No, he wanted to run off with her. To sip coffee over a heartfelt, balky talk about first loyalties and second chances, to trade pauses and bold looks at the bottom of each other's thinking, down to what he was pretty sure the universe had planned for the two of them. Instead he said, Okay.

Walt, she turned to a man he hadn't noticed. This might work out for both of you. The man sat in a corner with a felt pen, correcting hundred-pound sacks of beans that had been stenciled G-R-O-A-N in Washington. He was of average height, with small hands and feet and a blonde mullet. He wore Levi's and work boots, T-shirt and flannel shirt and baseball cap, but his eyes were something else. His eyes were the blue of a beer-commercial trout stream. With long, slender fingers and a lopsided, slightly goofy grin, he extended his hand.

Walt Blankenship.

The phone rang, and La Doctora reached out. Food Bank, can I help you? Just a minute, please. She looked up at El Pájaro. Walt will show you what to do, Miguel, but wait, don't you have a nickname?

He muttered that people called him El Pájaro, then gritted his teeth at their smiles: that means the bird, hunh?

Dazed, when they hit the sidewalk, El Pájaro looked back over one shoulder, then left, right. Walt seized him by the elbow and steered him to a peeling-paint Datsun pickup. You wanna have supper with us? El Pájaro nodded, speechless, and climbed into the passenger seat. Walt took two lefts and pulled into the Cascade Way Trailer Court, a maze of blacktop streets and awnings, carports and plastic wading pools, porch swings and wheelchair ramps. Walt parked. El Pájaro stepped down, cautious as an astronaut.

Onto the next-door patch of grass, a neighbor threw an automobile wheel and nodded at Walt. The neighbor was tall, shirtless, and red-haired, his skin a savage white with freckles. A gold film of body hair on him glowed in the afternoon light as he bent down, arranging charcoal briquettes around the wheel's inside rim. Then he produced an aluminum refrigerator rack and looked up at Walt and grinned, Hot dogs.

Go for it, Walt shrugged.

Up two Astroturfed wooden stairs, the screen door opened on a woman with large hazel eyes, sloping shoulders. I'm Imogene, Walt's wife.

She led him to a table. No two of the plates matched; the forks were aluminum. A centerpiece peanut butter jar held water and a handful of violets. She handed him a plate of slaw and mashed potatoes, and another to Walt.

Tell me, what do you miss about living in Mexico? she smiled.

El Pájaro blinked, and the words were out before he knew it. Ni madre. I don't miss a goddam thing about it.

She set a cardboard bucket of fried chicken between them.

Dig in, said Walt.

But Imogene was puzzled. Don't you want to be among your own people?

El Pájaro studied the face on the cardboard bucket, El Viejito. Little fat white guy with a beard sold chicken all over the goddam country. Pardon?

She took a deep breath. You're a full-blooded Mexican, right?

I guess.

You guess?

It's not like I did anything—a cautious tone—except I got born where I was. But if I gotta choose between pride and shame, well, you know.

She opened her mouth to reply, but a bell went off, and she turned to a microwave, then to a cupboard, T-shirt tight over her shoulders and lats, and produced a coffee cup, which she handed him along with a wedge of pie. He blinked when she extended her arm, and the triceps leaped out, forearm rippling. She had a massive jaw, a cupid-bow mouth, and a behind that your eyes just automatically followed, until Walt noticed him noticing. El Pájaro fixed his eyes on El Viejito. That crafty, old-man smile on freeway billboards.

The screen door crashed open. A skinny kid of twelve or so rushed into the room, whirled, and studied it. He had sandy hair, feet and front teeth too big, and the cautious, dreamy look of an astronaut. He seemed to be talking to himself. Then he raced back out the door and vanished around a row of parked cars.

Soooooonneeeee!!!! Blue cords stood out on Imogene's neck when she called her son. Soooooonneeeee! He reappeared in the doorway. Supper, she said out of the corner of her mouth.

When she turned back to her guest, Sonny edged up to the table and seized two drumsticks. He stuck one in his pants pocket, sat, and began gnawing the other, ignoring the plate of mashed potatoes and slaw his father slid in front of him.

Meet Sonny, Imogene said, without taking her eyes off El Pájaro. He's twelve, and he wets the bed and plays with matches.

Jesus! Walt let out a long breath.

Pardon me? El Pájaro said.

I said he wets . . .

Aaah, yes, El Pájaro raised one hand. He turned to the kid. Hola, Sonny. How you are?

Sonny's face looked surgically rebuilt, that was how expressionless it was. He continued chewing. He might have been watching whales mate, or a mummy getting peeled.

From her first marriage, said Walt.

Then Imogene, My ex was such a slob—a trucker, right?—he bathed once a week, and never washed clothes. He hung a urinal cake in the cab when the smell got too fierce.

El Pájaro said no thank you to another piece of chicken.

Can I be excused? Sonny was half out of his chair. He ground his teeth and shimmered with nervous energy.

Nope, said Walt.

Imogene's anger appeared to veer off in a fresh direction. Sonny acts out at school. They phone, I gotta go get him. Because of him, I had to quit my job at the nursing home.

A pause, as she and Walt looked at each other. They seemed to make a decision.

Imogene began. We, ummm, we wondered if maybe you needed a place to stay for a while.

Thing is, Walt said, you watch Sonny a couple hours a week, you sleep in our utility room free.

Sonny looked from one adult face to another. Without changing expression, he rose and, with a flick of one knee as he left the table, tipped the chair over behind him. El Pájaro said he thought it was a marvelous idea.

※   ※   ※   ※   ※

The First and Last Chance Tavern sat at the edge of town—where else?—with sagebrush out one window, and a trailer park out the other.

Not exactly a family place, said the bartender.

El Pájaro and Walt were straddling stools, cold draft in hand, after unloading pallets in hundred-degree heat.

But not like down at the Frontier, said Walt, with all those old guys sipping white port and milk and . . .

They call theirselves Deadpecker Row, the bartender finished his sentence for him.

Walt glared at the guy. El Pájaro nodded for another round, and Walt snuffled and spat black stuff in a bandana.

Nasty shit, the bartender ventured.

Enter an elderly gentleman, tall and thin in faded T-shirt and suspenders, with a knife-edge crease in his trousers. He wore a Panama hat that looked like somebody recently took a bite out of the brim.

Afternoon, Suitcase—the bartender, and then, from the corner of his mouth—talk about Deadpecker Row.

Reconnaissance, explained the elderly gent, peeking at the contents of the cooler behind the bar. He snapped off a dapper salute, extracted a white handkerchief, passed it over the barstool next to Walt, and perched. Whatta ya got?

Like it the fuck matters what I got? The bartender threw up his hands. You gonna order animal beer, aincha?

Please, said the elderly gentleman.

Walt turned to him. The guy beamed. Out of nowhere, he launched a bit of political analysis, which had him saying, within three sentences, No goddam president, doncha see, no real choice since 1948. Ever heard a Tom Dewey? Silence. He knocked back half a beer at a gulp. Talk about a gangbuster, a real gangbuster—Suitcase let fly a soulful belch—you know how come he lost in '48? More silence. Every criminal in the country voted against him is how come.

Walt finally clucked his tongue. Lost the criminal vote, hunh?

Suitcase, goddammit—the bartender, emerging from the men's room— leave the customers alone.

I'm a customer, said Suitcase.

Walt leaped to his feet with a shriek. He spun the old guy's stool like a condiment server. How about you leave us the fuck alone? Walt was opening and closing his fists.

Suitcase rose, adopting a high school principal's grin. He flatfooted the rest of his beer and took a step backward, palms out, then another. At the doorway, he spoke evenly, without hurry. Walt, I think you are a human skid mark.

Walt was near tears. He leaned back and stared at an elk head the size of a Volkswagen. His voice turned inside out. He told El Pájaro about a certain three-day drunk, a time when the old man burned his wife's clothes and locked Walt out of the house. The old man piled every bit of her clothing on the driveway and poured gasoline on it. Then he took her by the arm into a bedroom, came back out with the shirt and jeans and underwear she was wearing, and handed them to Walt. Along with a box of wooden matches.

El Pájaro asked, What did you do?

I slept on the driveway.

And?

It got cold.

Sliding two schooners in front of them, the bartender retreated, answering the phone, "First and Last."

Walt rubbed his eyes. Sonny's medication quit working a couple weeks ago.

Oh?

Yeah, we came home and found where he buried the neighbor's cat in our backyard.

Hey Walt, said the bartender.

But Walt paid no attention. Sonny didn't smother the cat. Walt was whispering. He left its head sticking out, and then fired up the power mower.

Excuse me, Walt—the bartender now, wiping both hands on his apron—it's Suitcase on the phone.

Now what?

He wants to know can he come back in?

We were just leaving, said El Pájaro.

One last round? said Walt.

The next-to-last round is what we say in Mexico, said El Pájaro.

How come?

El Pájaro said he didn't know. I guess because we're superstitious.

The next morning, a swath of sunlight inches across white enamel, a floor tile, the corner of an inflatable mattress, and he's awake. He takes his first breath of the day, stretches, wiggles his fingers and toes—then freezes. Voices six inches from his head. So the sunlight wouldn't wake him at an even earlier hour, he lay down with his head at the foot of the air mattress, which left his head exactly three inches from the laundry room's uninsulated wall, 3 3/4 inches from the voices of Imogene and Walt.

Wanna hand me that lighter, thanks, mmnnnnh. The voices are low.

You smoke that shit all the time.

Not true, and what's your problem?

Don't make me say it.

Okay, you seen my underwear?

I am tired of your selfishness is all. Under the dresser. Use the ashtray, please.

Sometimes I forget how come we're together.

We're together because we were indiscreet on a golf course one night.

That is not what I mean.

And when your cousin the groundskeeper turned on the lights, you started crying.

See what kind of stuff you remember? No wonder I feel like I do. You seen my socks?

You got 'em on, lover, and it was my uncle.

The one in Walla Walla for cooking meth?

Accessory to.

Anyhow, that night, you and me, wow, we fit each other like wings. People wanted to applaud, I could tell. I felt like, relief, because I just met the main guy in my life, which is Mr. You.

The arm under El Pájaro's head is numb; his nose itches. Then a drop in tone catches his ear.

Anything you wanna tell me? Right through the wall, the drag of stuff unspoken.

I mean it when I say I love you, Walt.

Good, but does Sonny know?

That I love you?

Very funny—does Sonny know you're gonna start fucking Miguel?

What?

Does he know or doesn't he?

Who?

Does Sonny know you're fucking Miguel, goddammit?

What kinda question is that?

Does he know?

I don't think so.

You make me sick.

Ten minutes later, they're acting like two completely different people, inviting El Pájaro to breakfast, insisting. The three of them crowd into the pickup, headed for breakfast, when Imogene says, I vote for IHOP.

Walt looks at her. You got your cell phone?

Hip pocket.

Turned on?

I got it so it buzzes my ass, okay?

The 10 a.m. sun rebounds off a windshield. Nobody says anything, and they pause at a traffic light.

I like the French toast with blueberry syrup, Imogene adds.

Because you know what they said—poor Walt can't leave the topic alone—I mean about the school phoning us. Any time during school hours, right?

But I always ask first, Imogene says, 'cause if they don't got blueberry syrup, I order the Belgian waffle with extra maple.

You little bitch, Walt whispers the words.

So fast it looks like a shrug, Imogene hits him in the solar plexus. Walt parks, slumps, opens his door and walks across the IHOP parking lot. Imogene follows, taking El Pájaro's arm. She smiles.

I can explain the menu if you want.

That afternoon, he rode with La Doctora out to a dining hall in the fields. Twelve guys, sweaty, just off work, waited on folding chairs.

El Pájaro looked away as she opened a metal box containing five purple, eight-inch dicks. They had veins and everything. The guys on folding chairs before her shifted and squirmed, unable to look at each other, let alone at that much anatomical correctness. The next few minutes lasted forever. El Pájaro was there to interpret, although there wasn't much to say. The lesson consisted of watching a video, then learning how to put on a condom correctly, with no wrinkles or air pockets.

Fíjense, El Pájaro addressed the guys, dealing out a dozen tinfoil-wrapped condoms like they were cards.

Then La Doctora handed one of the dicks to a sixteen-year-old, who leaped backward, steadied himself, and looked ready to cry. Without a word, a middle-aged guy seized the thing and peeled a wrapper. La Doctora passed among the chairs, observing as the men practiced. She paused in front of a guy missing one hand—he wore a huge black mustache and a look of wary pride, until La Doctora pointed to a nearly invisible air blister right above the purple foreskin and patted him on the shoulder. She bent over and picked up a tinfoil wrapper. She looked at her watch and nodded, and El Pájaro began packing up. As the guys finished, they nodded thanks and filed out, each with a food bank box of Maseca, rice, and beans.

Reluctant to make two trips, El Pájaro staggered into the parking lot, arms full. He nicked one corner of the monitor on the trunk lid and quickly looked over one shoulder. His head was spinning. When La Doctora and he sat in the front seat, she clicked her seatbelt. Then she clicked his. She looked over at him, voice tired.

Thanks. I told you it was difficult. I appreciate your coming.

She still had those gray eyes, and her nose wasn't exactly crooked, only one nostril a little bigger. She had very even, very white teeth. She ponytailed her hair, pulled it through the back of a faded Cle Elum Fire Department baseball cap. You Light 'Em, We Fight 'Em, it said. Then, behind a pair of dark and streamlined lenses, she pulled out of the parking lot, around a twenty-year-old Chrysler Imperial, engine missing so bad it panted like a dog. When she waved at the four guys in it, El Pájaro didn't know how to feel. She turned onto a blacktop. Hayfields stretched out. He started to ask a question, then caught himself.

What? she glanced at him. Look, I'm sorry, her voice picked up momentum. That has to be done. We're talking about people's lives.

He looked out the window, and she turned on the radio. Back and forth in the fields, hundred-foot lengths of aluminum irrigation pipe reminded him of an uncle who came back dead from Califas after the pipe he carried touched a high-tension line.

One little bump, he heard himself say, and you're in the other world.

What's that supposed to mean?

My uncle got killed carrying irrigation tubes.

Pipes?

Yeah, he got . . . electrocuted? It used to happen all the time.

She pulled up in front of a taquera, a pickup-camper combo with awning and hand-lettered billboard menu and lawn chairs. It was barely 1 p.m., and they were the first customers. There were bowls of chopped onion and cilantro, red sauce, and green sauce; the tiny perfect napkins fluttered. La Doctora studied the menu, moving her lips. Two vegetarian, please, she said to El Pájaro, and a chorizo and a Diet Coke.

He turned to the woman behind the counter, who swiped at a wisp of hair, eyed the state license plate on the car, and fixed him with an amused look. Then, as El Pájaro and La Doctora sat under the awning and chewed and sipped, and breathed in a mint-field odor, and watched a hawk ride an updraft, he tried to think of what to say. He wanted to tell her he knew how his uncle felt, zapped into the unexpected, but he was okay, he wanted to tell her. He needed time was all.

He couldn't see her eyes behind the shades, but when she patted her mouth with a napkin and said—her voice very calm—I'm sorry about your uncle, he nearly wept with relief. I am also very sorry, her tone never changed, that this country comes on so hard. When they get here, people feel . . .

Like they got no privacy? He shot her a glance.

I was going to say lonely. She wadded her napkin.

He followed her to the car, looking at her ankles. Her reply deserved a bit of thinking, no? He could feel his eyebrows at work. No, he was an asshole, and all of this was an exile of bad breath and crusty socks and road signs you couldn't read. People making a future out of patience and a sixth-grade education. And now for that crafty, insolent, peasant smile, if you please. Thank you.

Neighbor

Don Luis is rubbing his hands together, ready for a little conversation. After years of making layoff decisions, and laughing off the effect it had on him, as well as on the guys his decision threw out of work, nowadays don Luis—when he thinks about it—says that was how the world used to be. You got that way hiring crews to pick somebody else's land all your life. ¡Ay! how Luis used to charm people. He could make great ill will vanish—at least he acted like he could—with a quip, an apt refrán, or a golden oldie of a saying. Of which he is proud to say he has an inexhaustible number. For life has blessed him equally with prosperity and poverty, though not exactly in that order. Wary of dying penniless, he worked day and night, phoning and faxing, now and then launching a blasphemy that would blister lead. Up and down the trailer court, people remember him as tall and thin, with a thin mustache, and kind of nondescript. But ¡híjole! when don Luis approached you with a pink slip, he took up all the space there was.

Retired, Luis bought a trailer across from that of his youngest boy. He now wears pressed chinos, with a Washington State Cougars sweatshirt, and sees his granddaughters every day. And nowhere in the bearing of this genial senior citizen can you catch a hint of the hard-ass who sent so many guys down the road in tears. He is mild and taciturn. But he is death on pests. Dusted with DDT in 1942, just to get across the border, don Luis by now, on a bright afternoon sixty-five years later, likes to sit in his front yard teaching a grandson how to get rid of moles with a garden hose and an ice pick.

Almost Honest

When I try to take an historical view of myself, all that appears is a peasant educated beyond his station, a hillbilly mongrelized by the demographic hugger mugger people refer to as immigration. All of that shows up in my taste for incongruity, as well as for its homely twin, coincidence. Oppositions at work long before I was born made me what I am, which is a guy born in a Missouri town that got its name when a local named James Wilson offered free whiskey to everyone who would vote for naming the place after his former hometown of Springfield, Massachusetts. Springfield, Missouri, was the incongruity that resulted. It is hometown to Bob Barker and therefore de facto launch pad for fifty years of incongruity in the form of *Truth or Consequences* and *The Price Is Right*. And yet, for me, the peculiar overtones of Springfield owe, as well, to a large coincidence. Thirty years after getting born in Springfield, I went off to live in its sister city, San Pedro Tlaquepaque, three thousand miles away in Jalisco state, in Mexico. In other words, Springfield, for me, is one big tangle of feelings. *Forbes* magazine not long ago named it as having the most unreliable weather in the nation.

Fittingly enough, I got a refresher course, last fall, in tangled feelings. Right here in my own backyard, a long black plume rose, wavered, twitched, and then became the tail of a skunk. At the edge of my yard, a skunk was digging, making dirt and rocks fly with darting, weasel-family moves. It disappeared into what looked like a tunnel, then emerged at the other end, two feet away, digging furiously. Dirt flew. Rocks the size of my fist flew. I approached to within twenty feet, a distance at which local skunks frequently whirl and raise the tail, but not now. This one ignored me entirely. So I retreated to the deck and started taking notes. A very business-like skunk, I told myself, one who wouldn't take no for an answer: he or she worked with a comic, oblivious energy.

And there I sat. Scribbling, as transfixed as Robert Lowell, the shaky poet of *Life Studies*, in that poem "Skunk Hour." Hung up on Satan and Hank Williams, the guy's itchy self-consciousness makes him see in a skunk—because, he says, it won't scare—a counterpoint to what he is. He sees a creature autonomous, alert, and free of his own indecisive shivering. So I said to myself, hmmm, and vowed to treat my new neighbor with more respect. I figured my skunk was at least as resolved as Robert Lowell's. Returning, however, an hour later to find the tunnel deserted, and only six inches deep, with rocks fallen back in it, I had to conclude that my skunk had got disgusted and walked off. So I walked off. Such was the difference, I told myself, between a family like the Lowells—their history multiplied a thousandfold by the note-taking of strangers—and my own, a family full of blanks and abandoned projects.

Specifically, I'm one of tens of thousands of people who abandoned Missouri, Kansas, and the Dakotas, from 1930–1970, to descend on the Columbia Plateau. In the Yakima River watershed, it was orchards and hops and beet fields that drew the first generations of us. Others came to this particular valley because they found work, as I did, with the county's largest employer, a regional branch of the state higher education system. The point is, most of us got here via routes so devious and arbitrary that they still invite description.

But notice how my remarks keep telescoping into each other? Call it mood slippage, or attention deficit. My own peculiar mentality creates a world with a half-life of two or three sentences, one that snaps like a soap bubble. Those best adapted to that world are immigrants—or migrants, or some equivalent—by which I mean fringe dwellers with not-quite-legal lives, beings that fly under radar and disappear into crowds. In San Pedro Tlaquepaque, for example, the local variation took the form of bulky, gruff fellows with little to say. They were out every morning plodding the sidewalk in Nike warm-ups, then lunched on appetizers and tequila, and tipped waitresses with a knowing smile. They wore gold neck chains, and an aftershave lotion that neighborhood dogs fled from. They spoke—when they had to—in brusque, emphatic sentences. I never knew what they did for a living.

But I had a general idea. In those days, the level of theft in the country was such that French and Italian pickpockets, it was said, apprenticed in nearby Guadalajara, acquiring their technique from light-fingered locals. Everybody was filching, pilfering, and swiping. It was just a way of life. My buddy Raúl says that when he got a job at the gas company, delivering and collecting cylinders, on a route that took him past several hundred houses every day, it took him no time at all to see that the real money lay in collecting tanks nearly full—leaving full tanks in their place—then selling the leftover gas. The company tolerated no black-market monkeyshines, of course. You better sell it right back to the company. The unspoken motto of the place—en este trabajo hay que ser casi honrado—is something I recall now more than ever. In this work, you gotta be almost honest.

Now more than ever, I say, because my historical view catches these United States in a presidential primary season, those few, hopeful months when promises made—we don't yet know how they'll be broken—follow sweeping appeals to our sense of what we have in common. No wonder presidential politics has a sneaky and unsettling effect. Presidential politics is one of the very few games we all play together in this country. Sure, not many of us vote in presidential primaries. Only about half of us vote in the general election that follows, for that matter. But name something else—other than our wars, of course—that we all pay attention to, some common topic of conversation. Presidential primaries are as near as we ever come to having a national conversation. After the two major parties name their candidates, one tired grind takes over. All the possibilities that flourished months before wilt at the speeches of candidates whose differences are perfectly microscopic.

Primary fever is contagious, I had to explain, not long ago, to Raúl. ¿Que qué? Well, forty years ago I went around doorbelling the streets of Portland for Gene McCarthy—I'm of that vintage—so when my own private montage of presidential primaries unfolds, Wallace crumples in a parking lot, and McGovern says in that shaky voice that we haven't heard the end of Watergate. In primaries, I went on, the unexpected stuff leaps out. Unexpected stuff has gotten candidates killed and maimed, of course. And yet, the more tightly planned and guarded presidential campaigns become, the further we recede—in years, yes, but even more, in attitude—from the night some guy with a bullhorn voice let fly: Give 'em hell, Harry. I told Raúl I grew up with the baggy suits and cigar smoke and whiskey breath and bonfire rallies of Kansas City politics in the '40s. My grandfather was election commissioner during the last of the Pendergast regime. I remember that unmarked patrol car out front at night.

And ad campaigns nowadays? Raúl was curious.

Well, they represent a two-billion-dollar investment on the part of interest groups too devious to identify. When the TV pandits get to work analyzing the obvious, leveling grave pronouncements, telling the country what the country thinks about its candidates, a quality of low farce takes over, the political equivalent of itching powder and fart balloons. The polls fly back and forth for weeks, but nobody finds the right question to ask to reveal the mood of the country. Does the country undergo anything that could be called a mood, anyway? Okay, maybe not, but every four years, something unimaginably huge speaks through all those ballot boxes and voting machines. The message is never entirely clear, and electoral fraud has existed since the beginning, but whatever kind of collective thinking does emit those votes, it wields more power than any individual or group in the history of the planet.

Let us not kid ourselves. *Vox populi* is a Roman concept, one so archaic that it fumbles highly technical issues like cloning and global warming. Nevertheless, on a given night, twenty-three states report a change very few of us expected. The winners, in one party, a black man and a white woman, represent an aftershock that took a couple of centuries to arrive. On a sunny day with wind in the branches, and slush ankle-deep in the drive, while walking out to the mailbox, I have to conclude that a lot of hatreds that ran through this land have dried up. Maybe even healed? I'm on the phone, an hour later, chatting about Hillary Clinton with my mother. Mother was born three years before women could vote.

Then I go to Yakima for biopsy results. I expect nothing favorable, not after the sonogram, not after that look which flew like a cursor from doctor to technician. They saw a shadowy spot on the left front edge of my prostate, and a look went from one to the other. What I saw—and yes, I saw it, no kidding—flew like a bat, or a manta ray, black, slippery, and gone. It wasn't hard to recognize. Hmmm, well, well, pleased to meetcha. Could've guessed after pulling steady fives in the PSA department, and after my father died of prostate cancer. A moment of chilly fear—what about my wife?—and then I feel kind of honored, as if I had graduated, and now walked around in on a secret bigger than sex. I like it that nobody knows my secret—not that I am mortal, but rather that my shelf life is up for grabs. Out there beyond repentance, and second thoughts, and famous last words, it feels positively playful: my pet vanishing point. It's gonna get me outta here. Next stop, La Chalaca. Makes for a flattering camera angle, no?

I await news of CAT scan and bone scan—whether the tumor has spread—on a pink bench at the corner of Yakima and Hall, approximately one million late-model drab cars going by. And? Full fathom five, sport. Grin and bear it for the sake of these tales that accumulate, no? I wish. The sky goes bright and flat with indifference to me and my radioactive veins. An hour later, though, I'm letting the good news sink in. Whew! That was close. Now hold the Alzheimer's, please, Lord. I wanna leave with the lights on.

The morning before surgery, I sit watching '40s footage—wide lapels and gray, stubby cars, and tight smiles. That afternoon is all anesthetic. When I come to in a dim room—whee, alive in Yakima, Washington—first thing I recall is my old man's tale of a muggy August night in 1940s Yakima. He heard a tipsy female voice across a hotel courtyard, You are too the only cabdriver I ever screwed. A moment later, I recall a sign outside an academic department I worked in for forty years. Please don't spit tobacco in the water fountain. Then I decide that both remarks are examples of how to be almost honest about tangled feelings, if only my own.

Now a foot of snow grips my yard, and thermometers drop to zero at night. Deer ransack a box of apples I left on the deck for them. I go days without getting out of the house, mainly horizontal, weak, bored. The little bladder dribbles they assured me would go away are doing just that, but I still wear pads, and changing them leaves me gritting my teeth. It's simple: I can't bear the smell of my own pee. The odor shames and threatens me. My reaction owes in part to memories of nursing homes—but wait, there's a fierce edge to that smell, something it takes days to identify, and then, bingo. My poor little pee pads give off a zoo aroma, specifically that of big cats. In fact, they smell like a certain clownish, playboy lion in the Morelia zoo. His paws are huge, that last inch of tail twitches, and how about those big, yellow, impersonal eyes? This morning, what rushes off my saggy body with its purple, six-inch scar? Odors of lion cage and mouthwash.

Because, lest we forget, this is a tale about a guy lying on a sofa letting his guts heal. He is practicing the relativism of looking at himself from across the room, trying to hear himself in the second person, but his mind wanders. Then one day, his mind doubles back through a floor-wax gleam, and zas he says hello to a guy on a couch, but you get the point. Somebody else lies there opened up, revealed down to the last minor distraction: in the 10 a.m. cottonwood shadows, crows are rasping at each other.

The crows mew and oink and growl. They yammer. They yammer until I think, why not? And so I proceed to nominate the crow as
the official bird of illegal immigration. Think of it! Patron of the life
undocumented, underpaid, and anonymous. But it makes sense. Sure,
the national seals of both the United States and Mexico feature the
eagle, that imposing scavenger. But let the crow represent something
else. Let the crow represent not supremacy but instead the raw altera-
tion and modification that keep us alive. After all, crows never stop
watching and talking. Collectively, they are a gigantic, squawky band-
width that runs in all which directions at the speed of sound with news
of roadkill and the like.

No wonder we live in a world overrun with crow info! The word
crow itself, on Google, triggers thirty-two million hits—a large and
expressive slice of collective thinking, one that recalls Jim Crow laws
and the phrase "as the crow flies," not to mention the practice of eating crow and a certain Indian agency in Montana. Consider how the
male crow approaches the female with fluffed feathers, with strutting
and fly-bys, and then they mate for life, and take turns sitting on the
eggs, producing a chick so adaptable that, at younger than twenty-six
days, it will imprint on anything that moves. They fly off with bits of
glass, rings, keys—the earth, to crows, must glitter like one big yard
sale. While protecting them at night from predators, their color, by day,
makes them visible to each other. They eat eleven ounces a day of bugs,
worms, mice, berries, and corn. And anywhere they eat, they post sen-
tries. Crows are so private that human beings, without some DNA,
can't even tell the males from the females.

The crow's nervy adaptability—or the human counterpart to it—
that was what Michel de Crèvecour admired about the young United
States. A French immigrant farmer in New York state in the 1790s, he
wrote that, among the citizens around him, three classes predominated.
People from New England were plain, thrifty, industrious types who
tended to disregard the social class you were born into, judging you,
instead, by the work you performed, or didn't. They frowned on excess.
They were remarkably good at business, at long-term planning. It was
their patience that brought the Industrial Revolution, first, to their corner of the country.

People from the South were different. The South was a society so
class-ridden that the well-to-do developed a taste for Walter Scott's nov-
els and the feudal worldview they were set in. The wealthiest planters

lived worlds apart from both their African slaves and the white yeoman who performed skilled labor. The wealthiest Southerners imitated Old World aristocrats in their dress, education, and avoidance of the commercial manufacturing bent of their cousins to the north. Meanwhile, poor whites reconciled themselves to a static life, one without the upward mobility bubbling all through New England. And if they didn't reconcile themselves, they packed up and left.

Where did dissatisfied white folk go? Why, they went to the nearest land unclaimed by other white folk, to what people were already calling the frontier. Soon enough, they were joined—in what would become Pennsylvania and Ohio, Kentucky and Tennessee—by several hundred thousand Scotch-Irish immigrants, refugees from the very institutions the wealthy planter class revered with all its might. The immigrant Scotch-Irish and the dissatisfied native born, those two strains are what form de Crèvecour's third group, people gathered at the frontier's edge, ready to launch themselves west into what remained of the rest of the continent. They would be the reason why, a bit more than two centuries later, we hear Arkansas vowels in what a Kansas fry cook says, why wheat farmers outside Spokane talk in the nasal, clipped tones of Harry Truman.

De Crèvecour's third group generated the culture of log cabin and flintlock, of the backwood still and the fiddle that sounds like bagpipes. They were a fidgety outfit, testy, impulsive, clannish. De Crèvecour marveled at their reluctance to settle down. Land was cultivated, he wrote, and the republic made prosperous, by a later phase of English-speaking immigration, a more responsible folk who promptly felled the girdled trees, plowed out the stumps, and built a house where the cabin stood.

People in de Crèvecour's third group, by now called hillbillies, arrived in the Columbia Plateau in the half century preceding World War II. They irrigated their orchards and their hop fields, and soon were sowing and harvesting winter wheat. Their grandchildren have become the majority population into which Mexican immigrants nowadays blend and, to the surprise of both, discover that their values are nearly identical. Of course, when they aren't, adjustments get made. Something about one misfit knowing another, maybe even a code shared by rejects. Their innate whatchamacallits pick up on each other.

That certainly is what happens when Raúl and a couple of friends and I convene the tertulia that meets in my backyard under a big umbrella: Barrio Unido de Exiliados en Yanquilandia. In meetings as frequent as they are unplanned, with wide-ranging discussions and cold beer, we blend the sacrament of confession with Toastmasters International. Because we feel a certain way of life collapsing in all directions, the stories we trade work like splints and splices. One night, the delegate from Windy City Carwash addresses an aspect of wildlife management. You blend a big garlic clove with a shot of olive oil, he reports, let it sit a couple days, then spread it on your pant cuffs before you take off across a certain well-known stretch of Arizona desert, and jíííjole the rattlesnakes flee your every step. The delegate from General Landscaping counters with a rendition of the dressing-down he had to give some pinche Hindu guy in L.A. who hired him for yard work, and then scolded him, even snapped his fingers at him. In the course of the tale, the delegate doubles back, sidetracks, and narrates from several different angles a concluding scene in which he, the delegate, launches the guy's tools into a hedge and stalks off. The enthusiasm of membership is apparent.

Then one morning, Bill Tremblay phones and mentions in passing that banks and sub-prime lenders have half-destroyed the country. That night, my own sweet Mrs. allows as how electoral fraud in 2000 and 2004 is wound in with the 9/11 attacks and international oil money. And me, well, I get dizzy. I'm surrounded by overviews, by analyses that have huge impersonal forces exercising unlimited power through money and glossy lies. In many regards, my life is that of a typical retired U.S. academic, wired into PBS and *The Times* and the *New Yorker*. However, I'm lucky enough to have a couple of hundred friends who worked like hell to enter, and to remain in, this land of invisible money and glossy lies. Most of them come from three thousand miles south, and certainly don't think they inhabit any paradise. It's better than where we come from, they say with a shrug. And yet, migod! what kind of endorsement is that? What about the outrage I share, most of the time, with Bill and my wife?

Okay, consider the perspective that my buddy Raúl turns on this country. He prunes trees and mows lawns, and for Raúl, this country is a godsend, an amazing opportunity. My point is this. I have to assume that Raúl's perspective is every bit as discriminating as that of Noam Chomsky, don't I? You mooncalf—the scrap of academic left in me sputters—are you comparing what goes through the mind of an immigrant hourly wage earner to the hyper-disciplined thinking of Noam Chomsky? Maybe, and maybe not. I certainly am contrasting the assumptions each makes about what is worth paying attention to. They couldn't be further apart, a pair of lives as different as those of Raúl and Chomsky. What matters very little to one is fiercely important to the other. Neither has ever heard of the other. Neither could imagine the other's life.

And there you see the double-jointed relativism I practice while my guts heal. Burning apple wood from orchards outside Yakima, putting out spoiled food-bank apples for deer at night, I wake to nothing but scraps, round black scat, and hoof prints shaped like vulvas—ullp, recalling what the surgeon said. No reason not to resume a normal sex life, he said, once you're healed. But hold on, migod, you know—I mourn them already, the brick sidewalk and dogwood blossom and tight skirt that took my breath away fifty years ago, or night air full of pollen and radio stations. Sex or lovemaking, the marriage act or just plain doing it, no matter what your terminology, it outran words. The act itself was irreducible, a molecular tension that held the world together. To say goodbye to all that? To a disheveled hotel room fifty feet below cathedral bells on a Sunday morning? Goodbye? No way. I decide to believe the doctor.

And the gnarled apple wood releases warmth in all directions, and clouds inch across the skylight. And raw gratitude takes over. At the door of an abandoned garage for municipal busses in the Bronx, thirty years ago, milkweed shoots rose through cracks in the concrete, and I was grateful. Twenty years ago, when my father and my first granddaughter died on the very same day—him in a Houston cancer ward, and her, two days old, in her mother's arms in Indiana—and willow branches took on that unearthly yellow glow they acquire in March, my glee was positively scary.

Bill and my wife and I inhabit a world made of assumptions. No argument there, but the trouble is, our assumptions about human behavior provide us with concepts and terms better adapted to condemning the life of Adolph Eichmann than to praising that of Anne Frank. Self-interest trumps altruism every time, we assume. And even when it doesn't, everybody else—we assume—assumes that fear and greed are more than a match for empathy. The more pessimistic our assumptions, however, the more uncomfortable I get. Something about any too-knowing tone gets under my skin, especially the tone of experts who claim acquaintance with the darker edge of human nature. It's not exactly that I think they're wrong. Rather, I'm suspicious of their motives. The world view of Chicken Little is very attractive to people hoodwinked and condescended to—people, I have to admit, like Bill and my wife and me.

In contrast, I didn't feel the least bit hoodwinked and condescended to on the weekend my buddy Raúl announced that he had to drive to California to pick up his sister Nata and his niece, plus two of their friends. They were coming into the country wet as the day they were born, and Raúl had his license suspended. When he went to rent a van, they wanted a credit card as security, so could he borrow mine? Sure. And then I said, what the hell, lemme drive, and thought no more about it. But once headed south on Interstate 5 with coffee and CDs, I found myself repeating cheeky incantations. Who the hell was the Department of Homeland Security to be telling me who got into my country and who didn't? Chickenshit cruelty on the part of a few thousand politicians, I kept telling myself. Meanwhile, Raúl kept calling, as scheduled, and the woman who was crossing Nata and Co. never answered.

We showered and showed up at 3 a.m. at the San Bernardino apartment complex they said to, and sure enough, Nata and friends yawned and picked up their suitcases. The woman who had crossed them—La Coyota, let us call her—was cheerful, good-looking, in her thirties, and all business. She took Raúl in the kitchen, where he proceeded to peel off hundred-dollar bills. She hadn't answered her phone, she said, because of having dropped it in a mud puddle two days before. Nata later told me that La Coyota's father was also in the business of smuggling people, but La Coyota had nipped across the street and undercut his price by $200.

Nata had set out in shower thongs. The first time they tried to sprint that hundred yards of desert, from one country to the other, Nata fell and got pulled from under a juniper bush on some family's front lawn—a migra spotted her ponytail sticking out—and the others came out meekly. He hauled off all five to be printed and processed and bussed back across the border. For the next attempt, three hours later, La Coyota lent Nata a pair of Kmart tennies, which Nata now returned. Soon as I run them through the washer, said La Coyota, they're ready to cross the border again.

Anyhow, we climb in our rented van, and the sunrise catches us headed north out of L.A. through cut banks and pink hills. The first time we stop for gas, I notice a chubby kid, maybe twenty, who comes out the door of a convenience store, tapping a pack of cigarettes on her palm, just in time to see the guy she apparently spent the night with pulling away in his pickup. The grin peels off her face, and what is left is unbearable to look at. She is both ashamed and getting used to being ashamed. The whole thing takes maybe twenty seconds. What hurts is the ordinariness of it. Followed by ten hours of Interstate 5.

In a rest area in northern California, ten hours later, I'm walking back and forth through strips of sunlit grass. There's maybe a hundred people around, strolling, tugging leashed dogs, unwrapping sandwiches, paying no attention to me or my passengers. I'm woozy after five hundred miles of driving, legs and neck stiff, fingers cramping from the steering wheel. As if I were watching myself from miles off, I know I'm committing a felony that could get me—later, I do check it out—a total of sixty years in prison. The federal statue provides ten years per passenger for anybody who transports or moves or attempts to transport or move aliens within the United States. I know this is serious business, but the idea won't focus. I feel, on the contrary, that I radiate a secret. A feeling of indescribable power nearly leaves me giggling. Me, I've got the drop on all these dog walkers and sandwich nibblers. I'm undercover, you could say. I know stuff they don't. It gives me a huge, invisible leverage.

For some reason, that feeling blinked off the moment we crossed the Oregon border. That was when it occurred to me that the whole weekend had been a lesson in being almost honest, nothing more. After all, I had to choose between two loyalties—to my friend, yes, and to my country—in circumstances that called for a snap judgment. Mine was a reflex reaction, nothing more. Hell yes, I chose to help my friend, and probably would do so again. Though I'm not proud of what I did, I'm not exactly ashamed of it either.

But above all I have to admit, in retrospect, that the story makes me look disdainful and self-important. I look like a sniffy do-gooder mocking the work of the Border Patrol and immigration reformers alike. For all of which I apologize. I didn't mean what I did as a form of protest, not at all. Politics played no part in my motives—or at least no more than it did in those of Raúl.

I'm tempted to attribute what I did to the confianza I share with Raúl, but English, alas, offers no equivalent to the word confianza. The term refers to a binding power people develop, an especially Latino trust or faith or confidence—grown over time—in somebody else. That people who speak English get along without such a term, by the way, says a great deal about people who speak English.

Related, somehow, to my argument is a plain linguistic fact: the term confianza is used also to refer to a distinction in grammar, specifically, whether you're addressing the listener as usted or as tú. The phrase hablar de confianza refers to use of the tú form of verbs, but the difference between tú and usted doesn't exist in English. In English, the difference between the two pronouns collapses, and what emerges is one bedraggled, indeterminate you—a pronoun so noncommittal that it won't even change its form in the plural.

English, in other words, doesn't require that you declare with every verb the degree of trust you think exists between you and the person spoken to. And Spanish demands that you do so. The overall effect? English offers a kind of neutrality, a chance to obscure, if not your feelings, then at least the degree of distance you feel between you and the person you're talking to. No wonder so much folklore tells us that English-speaking people are more reserved than those over-loyal and way-too-demonstrative folk who speak Spanish. And just why is it that the term confianza has no counterpart in English? Maybe because it refers to a tone of voice that lies beyond the hearing range of English speakers. That is indeed a snide remark, but made in English, you will notice. And by a fellow who chooses to live where English is receding.

Whatever change is about to happen out here, it will be both surprising and very old. No wonder that skunk tunnel gave off a lesson in tangled feelings. Lava formations, according to NASA, make where we live look like the surface of Mars.

As Told To

I began with an ordinary but open-ended question: how come, at retirement age, I wind up spending most of my time with young families caught up in el flujo? They confide in me, yes, and I keep scribbling notes about them, but what is the mutual attraction? True, they value certain character traits emphasized in my childhood. With Ike, they share an edgy vulnerability, one that expects you to get through life the best way you can. But beyond their common reverence for el aguante, for plain forbearance, the trait that binds hillbillies and mexicanos is this: we're the kind of people who answer a question with an anecdote, a moment trimmed to fit the occasion. Because the anecdote is our fundamental unit of thought, we develop an appetite for turnover, for life as a string of anecdotes. No wonder we migrate.

Sam Johnson defined the anecdote as a minute passage of private life. The term began with Procopius, last of the classical historians, who entitled his last work *Anecdotes*. After two volumes of military history on the triumphs of Justinian, his emperor, and another book devoted to the emperor's public buildings, he set out on a very different piece. His title indicated that his subject matter—the hot scoop on imperial misbehavior—hadn't yet circulated in written form, however well known it was as gossip. An-ecdotai, they were, matters not yet released to the public. Does the title somehow indicate that getting written down changes gossip to history? Procopius's subject matter was cheating wives, palace murders, great lives viewed from an angle that made them seem ordinary, if not downright kinky. Fifteen centuries later, Victorian-novelist sensibility even managed to wring another tone out of the term anecdote, when Disraeli invented the noun anecdotage, referring to that stage of life—at which I find myself, of course—when the thinking of the elderly meanders. It is in our anecdotage when apparently independent scenes connect across time, q.e.d., the anecdotal slant to my reporting. What better topic for the anecdote monger than im/migrant life? Reporting el flujo, you substitute the incongruous for the kinky.

Anyhow, I grew up hearing tales, but until my friends moved into town, Ike's example was all I had, my only close-up of somebody lightin' out for the territories. Everything changed when my friends arrived. This book is about a default setting I share with them, a meta-attitude that knits together apparently different kinds of people. A matter of preference, call it. Hillbillies and mexicanos demand a story without heroes or villains, with only visionaries and klutzes, and now and then a man or woman so brave your teeth ache. People like Ike and my friends always inhabit the beginning, somewhere with room to make what you want of both yourself and what you entered the world with. In other words, Ike, that avid homesteader, was fueled by the same blend of opportunism and optimism as someone who only yesterday paid $2,000 to cross the border.

Optimism and opportunism are qualities not often mixed. The effect is much praised, and it should be, though Ike and my friends also share the downside of their ambition. They become unbearably self-conscious. My friends fidget and blunder. They lose documents and show up late for appointments. They simply cannot imagine what they look like to a social worker, court-appointed attorney, or building inspector, and therefore go to great lengths to avoid mixing with Anglo officialdom. Their wariness recalls how sensitive Ike was to the figure he cut—or thought he did—in the eyes of the county health officials, that railroad bull, and the landlady who wouldn't permit harvesting on Sunday. My friends and Ike share a strong distaste for looking foolish.

Imagine some Fourth of July afternoon when the TV releases images of New York Harbor, the Statue of Liberty, Emma Lazarus—the whole official scenario about this being a nation of immigrants, etc. Remember that my friends, whichever side of the border they were born on, could care less what some New York rich lady said about huddled masses and wretched refuse. And you know why? Because immigration telescopes into migration, because arrival dissolves into travel: one minimum-wage job to another. And was it any different for Ike? Yes, but not much. That feisty homesteader attitude barely survived the tedium of being a tenant farmer. Our Grover Cleveland–era newlywed became an unshaven failure laid out back in Missouri in what they used to call overhauls, surrounded by middle-aged children returned from wherever el flujo had deposited them. Hillbillies and mexicanos certainly aren't the only ones who preserve discouragement, frustration, helplessness, and regret in tales that call for long-term courage. But they do it damn well.

Anecdotal thinking breaks off without warning, of course. Most of the people we meet in anecdotes simply vanish. And as for updates, well, Carlos and Pera remain together. By now, she refers to him in conversation as ese hombre, and he to her as esa mujer. The neighbors, however, make a cradle-board shape with hand and forearm, and raise their eyebrows, and Pera and Carlos squirm. Meanwhile, local gossip lost track of Ward. No news of him since the day he was convicted and given fifteen years for setting the range fires that dimmed the sky that summer. Why the hell did he do it? Nobody knew. Community speculation has its limits, after all. Imogene, they say, moved to Las Vegas and took up lifting weights. But it was neighborly spite, and nothing more, that reported her at work in a casino dead-lifting a platform of several hundred rabbits for an Easter show. The same attitude reported Sonny was in juvie in Vegas for shoplifting an ice pick to relieve grade-schoolers of their lunch money.

El Pájaro died in a car wreck, I am sorry to report. I think of him every day. He hit a spot of black ice and wound up in the other world, people said. But from my own narrow perspective, what happened after he died belongs in a book about the feelings he brought out in people. In what passes around here for the normal turn of events, guys from El Pájaro's hometown showed up, importing new tales about him, some of which caught on, while others didn't. At some point raw momentum took over—who can resist a tale about a local hero, after all? The upshot was El Pájaro dissolved into anecdotes, stuff that had a half-life of months, if not weeks. Specific details blended and changed names. But that was a problem only if you recognized no turnover in your own thinking.

One version, especially, revealed the sneaky pride he still brings out in people like me, the tumbler click of knowing who you are, then acting without regret. Maybe only a couple of times in your life do you ever notice the unmistakable glow of anecdote breaking out from behind the sidewalks and faces around you. The day it happened to El Pájaro, ironically, he was working as a cop. Before devoting himself to the study of English, and to escaping his hometown, El Pájaro had accepted a politician uncle's offer of an appointment to the Policía Preventiva Municipal, the lowest paid and least trained and most maligned arm of the Mexican law. He sat through firearms training and a brief run-through of the statutes, and then took up foot patrol duties with his cousin Beto.

One Sunday afternoon, when he was alone and patrolling his hometown plaza, he watched glue huffers in an alley, raggedy-ass kids weaving, rolling their eyes. Then a skinny octogenarian, with pants unzipped and a pee stain, asleep under a park bench. Picture El Pájaro ready to faint from boredom. A little before 2 p.m., a hullabaloo arose across the plaza, as one drunk spit in another's food, and the offended party naturally set to work with a plastic fork on the face of the offender. But when El Pájaro appeared, jingling a pair of handcuffs, offended and offender alike vanished.

Nothing out of the ordinary. Dogs panted in the shade under pickups, and blue plastic tarps billowed. Sawhorse-and-plywood tables below them held the fruit and vegetables, extension cords, lightbulbs, plumbing parts, and kitchen doodads that people brought to sell, examine, or argue about: it was el tianguis. It was small-town Mexican private enterprise in its purest form. On a day of the week fixed by custom, several hundred people descended on the plaza, supposedly with commercial intent, but really to do the jawboning and gossiping demanded by civic continuity.

By 3:30 p.m. he had a headache. He took a deep breath and gritted his teeth. In the fruit rinds and bus exhaust and tarp shadows, he saw, stretching out, his own drab, small-town future, familiar, menacing. Years and years of kid shrieks and pigeon shit, of sullen drunks shooting him glances. But when his shift was an hour from ending, his cousin Beto pulled up with a cold six-pack on the dashboard of his peeling-paint Trans Am. The passenger door opened. Beto handed him a beer, and an awkward silence followed. Neither wanted to talk about the two-week suspension they both faced for what an official report, the week before, had called highly unprofessional behavior. Puras babosadas. The two cousins waved off what had happened as only another exercise in the wholly comic futility of law enforcement.

According to the report, the two had seen a man run into a cornfield at the edge of town. Both officers approached, drawing their weapons, but the suspect fled while the two argued which of them should carry the single bullet they had between them. The cousins swore each other to secrecy, of course, but somehow word got out, and now they sat in the Trans Am with Beto's collection of Sinaloa corridos and the airco blasting. They talked about painting the Trans Am, about Beto's pregnant girlfriend, about finding work in el norte—topics that brightened El Pájaro's thinking. He began to feel like himself again.

Three beers and fifteen minutes later, he stepped back on the sidewalk, a new man, with a new firmness in his stride. He radiated authority, in fact. He couldn't keep a smile off his face. At least not until he tripped over an elderly 'ñora at the curb. Into a twenty-gallon aluminum steamer, she was stuffing the few tamales she hadn't sold at the tianguis. Thud. Solid contact. The steamer and the 'ñora went flying. The tamales went plop.

The old lady leaped to her feet, calling him patán and naco. She cinched her rebozo, sniffing when he tried to apologize. But when she proceeded to wonder out loud what unspeakable acts of peasant sex had produced a creature like him, El Pájaro felt something give, and knew that he had hit his limit. He knew he had better head for el norte. And just so he wouldn't change his mind at some point in the future, he then proceeded to unzip and pee all over that lady's tamales. Because she, it turns out, was the aunt of el presidente municipal. So you can see why people like me would admire and repeat the tale for years. The Life and Times of El Pájaro. As told to, and by, practically everybody.

About the Author

A writer and community organizer, I am the author of three previous nonfiction collections. *Augury* (University of Georgia Press, 1992) was selected by Robert Atwan for the 1990 AWP Award for Creative Non-fiction. *Waiting for the Earth to Turn Over* (University of Utah Press, 1996) followed, and then *Because I Don't Have Wings* (University of Arizona Press, 2006). Retired from many years of alternating academic assignments in Mexico and the United States, I now work in a food bank in the Pacific Northwest. I am married, with four children and two grandchildren. By an historical accident, I am English/Spanish bilingual. I'm also convinced that migration and immigration are merely different phases in the same existence.

LaVergne, TN USA
30 December 2009

168598LV00002B/2/P